WHAT'S THE TIME IN CASABLANCA?

Travels in Europe and beyond

Ally Reid

Boxroom Publications: 2023

Cover design by: Art Painter
Library of Congress Control Number: 2018675309
Printed in the United States of America

To Fiona, Kathleen, and Sean, with love

Good company in a journey makes the way
seem shorter - Izaak Walton

CONTENTS

Title Page

Copyright

Dedication

Preface

Chapter 1: Well, That Was Stupid   1

Chapter 2: The Rest of That Trip   12

Chapter 3: Edinburgh to Mahón   20

Chapter 4: Edinburgh   29

Chapter 5: Porto and Aveiro   31

Chapter 6: Murça and Douro Valley   44

Chapter 7: Coimbra   51

Chapter 8: Guarda   55

Chapter 9: Salamanca   58

Chapter 10: Avila   62

Chapter 11: Sevilla   66

Chapter 12: El Puerto de Santa Maria   72

Chapter 13: Cádiz and Jerez   77

Chapter 14: Palma de Mallorca   80

Chapter 15: Sol del Este, Menorca   83

Chapter 16: Between Big Trips   89

Chapter 17: Edinburgh to Mahón   92

Chapter 18: Edinburgh   95

Chapter 19: Catania   97

Chapter 20: Lipari, Vulcano and Salina   100

Chapter 21: Stromboli   105

Chapter 22: Taormina   115

Chapter 23: Siracusa   120

Chapter 24: Ragusa   127

Chapter 25: Genoa and Portofino   131

Chapter 26: Genoa to Lisbon   137

Chapter 27: Sol del Este, Menorca   148

Chapter 28: Long-Haul Trips   153

Chapter 29: The Wonder of Tesco   163

Chapter 30: Toes Back in the Water   172

Chapter 31: Edinburgh to Mahón   183

Chapter 32: Rovinj   186

Chapter 33: Trieste   192

Chapter 34: Zadar   196

Chapter 35: Matera   199

Chapter 36: Athens   203

Chapter 37: Izmir (Ephesus)   207

Chapter 38: Istanbul   211

Chapter 39: Corfu   216

Chapter 40: Venice   220

Chapter 41: Verona   226

Chapter42: Palau   230

Chapter 43: Bonifacio   234

Chapter 44: Sol del Este, Menorca   239

Chapter 45: Back to the Future   245

Acknowledgement   249

PREFACE

When Fiona and I started out on our journey together in 1979, we had each previously been abroad only a handful of times. All of these trips were short holidays in various parts of mainland Europe.

As we have progressed through our life and travels together, we've continued an enduring love affair with the continent of Europe, with which the UK was engaged in a formal partnership until very recently.

Although further flung and perhaps more exotic destinations have grabbed our attention, and been duly visited and enjoyed, we've continually returned to this relatively small but hugely varied and appealing part of the world, particularly to the Mediterranean and its immediate environs.

We've progressed from setting forth and taking things as they come to a more studied and planned approach but one which still leaves room for some spontaneous decisions and deviations from the plan.

In writing this book, I've tried to pull together stories from our earlier trips and set our later travels against the backdrop of those formative experiences.

We may not have hacked our way through the jungles of Borneo or bungee-jumped off the Macau Tower in China. We both firmly believe, however, that you can design and experience your own personal exciting adventures at the level which suits you as an individual.

We've always loved to travel by train, even the one so crowded leaving Belgrade that I had to throw myself upon the mercy of the sardine-packed travellers who had spilled right out to the open doorway to our carriage.

Sea-going craft of a variety of sizes also feature, as marine travel is also a favourite of ours. This is despite our immediate family's penchant for dubious adventures on the high seas (well mostly rivers, lochs, and coastal waters!).

Like everyone else, Covid-19 put a spike in our well-laid plans, and we had to persuade ourselves that it was (almost) safe enough to get back in the saddle and start our travels once again. So we did, and long may it continue to be possible!

CHAPTER 1: WELL, THAT WAS STUPID

Latakia, Syria: October 1980

Ok, so maybe we should have taken better notice of the warning signs.

We are preparing to disembark from our Black Sea Shipping Lines boat onto the dockside of Latakia, the large port on Syria's Mediterranean coast. Our first ever steps on Middle Eastern soil, and indeed outside the confines of the continent of Europe.

Before we started out on our big trip across Europe to Egypt, we had inevitably conjured up in our minds how it would feel to land in various exotic locations, the like of which we'd never previously experienced.

My own daydreams of arriving in Syria had somehow involved images of Sydney Greenstreet in the movie "Casablanca" (despite the obvious fact that Casablanca is in Morocco). Sydney was strolling through a *souk*, wearing a white linen suit, a stylish silk cravat, and a white Panama hat.

He was bargaining with quiet confidence with the friendly and slightly obsequious local traders. Perhaps he purchased a fine inlaid walking stick, with a polished metal handle. At a fair price which kept everyone happy.

Most of all, the sun was shining down steadily on the top of Sydney's Panama hat, and the general atmosphere was exotic and relaxed.

Back in the real world, my girlfriend Fiona and I lean over the deck rail as we slowly approach the blackness of the dockside in Latakia. We begin to feel the all-enveloping, stifling heat of a Syrian evening on our faces. A very dark Syrian evening.

By way of context, earlier in the year, the infamous siege of Aleppo had taken place. This military operation was conducted by the forces of the Syrian government, led by Hafez al-Assad, during a period of armed conflict between Sunni groups and the al-Assad government. Government forces committed several massacres during this operation. An assassination attempt on President al-Assad failed in June 1980.

None of this had percolated into our consciousness in the lead-up to our trip.

As we enter the confines of the harbour, we both notice intermittent flashes of light and sharp cracking sounds. These emanate from the side of the dock opposite where we intend to disembark.

"D'you not think that looks and sounds like gunfire?" Fiona questions apprehensively. "Are you sure you want to go ahead and get off the boat?"

"Nah, we'll be fine. It's just fireworks," I reply, with all the self-assurance of a 25-year-old, who has previously been no further east than the Austrian Tyrol. "We can't come all this way and not get off the boat to see what the place is like, can we?"

21-year-old Fiona continues to look sceptical and apprehensive. She had previously been caught up in an ETA riot in San Sebastian, during which she had to take refuge by crouching in a shop doorway, trying to avoid the tear gas. Perhaps this experience has imbued her with a bit more common sense.

The wooden gangway is duly lowered with a clatter onto the dock, and we disembark. The air is an almost suffocatingly warm, dry blanket, after the airiness of the sea crossing from Cyprus. The Syrian night sky seems to enshroud us and is impenetrably black.

We carry with us some cash and our passports, but no cameras or any other valuables. The dockside is bleak and virtually deserted. Standing under a weak lamp, whose light barely seems to impact the blackness around us, stands a random-looking man. He points us towards a very large hanger-type structure. Passport Control, we reckon.

We step through the doorway into the hanger, in the company of a group of six chattering Polish people. They are the only other passengers who have disembarked from our Russian ship. We really should have drawn some intelligent conclusions from that.

Passing into the brightly lit hanger, we are instantly assailed by the noise, cigarette smoke, and body odours of literally hundreds of men. They are packed into the brightly lit interior, for we know not what reasons. Many of them seem to suffer from conditions of the eyes with which we were to become familiar in North Africa - distressing-looking infections, which may have resulted from the amount of sand in the air they routinely encounter. And presumably also due to a lack of good medical provision.

The arrival of some Europeans, three of whom are fair-skinned, blonde-haired females, obviously comes as a welcome diversion. The atmosphere is instantly intimidating. Comments are made from close quarters and terse-sounding questions are fired at us in Arabic, which we don't understand. The females in the party are closely scrutinised. We hurry on through the claustrophobic throng of faces, pressing towards the far exit.

When we finally make it to the exit door, our passports are given a cursory glance by another random-looking chap. We emerge once more into the open air, practically gasping with relief.

As our eyes adjust to the gloom, we realise that we have stepped into a large shanty town-type area, festooned with tents and open fires. Tea is being brewed, but our passage again attracts considerable attention, with more attempts at communication in staccato Arabic.

These overtures don't sound too friendly to our untutored ears connected to our, by now slightly panicky, Scottish brains. At this point, you may be surprised to learn that we do and did indeed have functioning brains.

We note fairly quickly that a number of the exclusively male population are carrying sub-machine guns. They're dressed casually in t-shirts and sweatshirts. Camouflage fatigues are *de rigeur* trouser wear. The men do not look like regular soldiers, but they do happen to be significantly armed.

We eventually turn out of the shanty area into a quiet but reasonably well-lit alleyway. We become aware of the looming shadow of a man behind us. His shadow is clearly carrying a sub-machine gun. We press on, shoulders hunched and brows slick with sweat, praying that he will mercifully lose interest.

We make it safely to the dock compound exit, in the wake of the six cheerful Poles. Passing through the huge gate we start to walk along a rough, dimly lit road, of indeterminate length, into the town. We should have researched this bit in advance.

Around fifty metres along the road stands an isolated café, with a veranda at the front, the whole structure raised on a small mound. As we approach the café, everyone within it seems to appear simultaneously on the veranda to stare - again an all-male welcoming party.

The biggest rat I have ever seen chooses that moment to run across the roadway directly in front of us and disappear into a drainage ditch. A look passes between Fiona and me which confirms that we have both reached the conclusion that discretion should form the better part of valour.

The last we see of the Polish contingent, they are still walking up the road in the direction of the town, chattering happily away to each other. We never spot them on board the ship again. Perhaps Latakia is so nice that they have decided to stay.

As we head back towards the gate which gives access to the docks, it dawns on us both that we'll have to negotiate our way back through the tents of the perilous shanty area, back through the humanity-crammed hangar, and onto the dockside where our boat is berthed. This thought gives rise to some degree of trepidation.

"I don't like it here!" says Fiona tremulously. "No, it's not good. Let's get back to the boat as fast as possible," says I, having lost all enthusiasm for exploration.

As we stride back up the alleyway, into the tented mini-village, we realise that mercifully our luck appears to be in. The aromas of roasting meat and frying bread waft towards us. We pass through the shanty area with little attention being paid to us - it is dinner time. The whole population is squatting, cooking, and eating.

We even spot a narrow path around the hangar, which avoids the need to re-run the gauntlet within the building. On the other side of the structure, we walk purposefully onto the dock and along the quayside to gaze up at the dark hull of our boat. The gangway has naturally been pulled up.

Latakia dockside is now treated to the pathetic sight of two young British travellers shouting up to the watch on deck. He initially refuses to lower the gangway for us to get back on board. We then yell, increasingly shrilly, whilst brandishing our British passports in the air, until he relents and allows us back up the plank to the sanctuary of the ship.

Once back in our large (six berth), but very basic, cabin we finally relax. There is no air conditioning and it's a still, hot night. We stretch out *au naturel* on our respective bunks with our reading material of choice.

There is a knock at the cabin door. We ignore it. The knocking becomes more insistent. Fiona covers herself up whilst I don a pair of shorts.

I open the door to be met by the friendly, grinning faces of two young men. "We are your roommates!" one exclaims enthusiastically.

Spooked by our very recent dockside experience, I mutter something along the lines of "That'll be right," and close the door. We get dressed and pick up our as-yet unpacked rucksacks and let the two chaps into the cabin, whilst we head for the Purser's Office.

When we get there, the crew member on duty doesn't seem surprised to see us. We surmise that he might be playing a little joke on us.

As I launch into the argument I have been preparing for us to get an unshared cabin to ourselves, he interrupts, in English with a heavy Russian accent, complete with a droll undertone:

"Perhaps sir and madam would like me to transfer them to one of our Superior cabins?"

"Yes please!" we intone in unison. A small amount of cash changes hands. It has to be small as that's all we have.

We are shown to another (four berth) cabin on another deck. Its interior wouldn't pass muster on any self-respecting cruise ship, but it has a porthole that seems to admit a little air, and we have it to ourselves.

We stretch out once more on our new bunks, to read a little, before turning in. Within a few moments, our neighbours across the hallway start to chant/sing. The Arabic incantations might be interesting in another setting at a different time of day, but as they increase in volume, so does our irritation.

We try to ignore the noise. It doesn't work. Eventually, Fiona snaps and starts battering the wall violently with a shoe, yelling "Please be quiet!" Or words to that effect. The singing stops abruptly. We settle down once more and drift off to sleep.

In the morning, I am nominated to leave our cabin to go to the lounge in which papers are being examined and passports are being stamped. I also need to answer the call of nature.

After the latter activity, I am returning to the cabin when two young men, who appear to have been waiting for this moment, emerge from the cabin opposite. Their approach radiates unfriendliness. One blocks the corridor whilst the other pushes me up against the wall. They are standing uncomfortably close. I have no idea how to say "Your singing was very tuneful last night," in Arabic.

"Give us soap," the more aggressive one demands. "Pardon?" says I, cleverly playing for time. "Soap to wash our hands," he expands, clarifying for the obvious idiot in front of him. "I don't have any," I answer truthfully.

"Are you American?", the more aggressive one suggests, his face inches from mine. "No!" I respond emphatically, exaggeratedly shaking my head for emphasis.

"English?" Once more my firm response is in the negative.

"Where are you from?" his mate demands, obviously tiring at the thought that the aggressive one might be only starting on a long list of countries of the world.

"Scotland," I declare. "Kenny Dalglish. Joe Jordan!" I exclaim, making "heading the ball" movements for emphasis, desperately trying to get my point across.

The mood instantly lightens. Both young guys relax and smile broadly. They break eye contact, touch their foreheads, and step aside to let me get to my cabin.

I nip in, lock the door, and breathe a huge sigh of relief. That's the first time that playing the Scottish card has ever actually worked when on the spot abroad, in line with the mythical stories one hears!

A short time later, our luxury cruise with the Black Sea Shipping Line is over, and we disembark at Alexandria. Good afternoon Egypt!

* * *

This, our first foray abroad for any length of time which exceeded a normal fortnight's holiday, was conceived within the first few months of our relationship beginning. I had graduated three years earlier, and since then had worked in a succession of crappy fixed-term office jobs. The trip was fixed to start shortly after Fiona's graduation in the late summer of 1980.

We did feel like we were being a bit adventurous, as none of our friends had ever attempted this type of trip before. In the years to come, such journeys became more commonplace, but we felt like trailblazers.

At the time, I was living in a flat in Tollcross in Edinburgh, with a good mate. Within ten minutes of me leaving the flat in a taxi, to pick Fiona up and head for Waverley Station, my mum had phoned my flatmate to check that I had packed a warm jumper.

In those far-off times, the Transalpino Ticket allowed cut-price rail travel across the continent of Europe. We decided to plan our route, but not to book any accommodation along the way. Fiona's faded orange Girl Guide tent was strapped to one rucksack, and we both took foam ground sheets. This was with the general intention of camping as much as possible. I had never camped in my life before.

We reckoned on staying an average of three days in each location, and our combined savings allowed for an overall budget of £5 per day, including accommodation, for a seven-week trip. It has to be said that, even in 1980, that was not a princely sum of money.

Rather than just stick within the confines of Europe, however, we had decided to be a little more ambitious. We wanted to visit Egypt and see the Pyramids, along with some of the country's other wonders. The flight back from Cairo was booked for around seven weeks after our departure date. It would be only the third time I had travelled by plane.

As we had enjoyed a romantic weekend in Paris together, earlier in 1980, we decided to start there. So it was a train to London, change stations, then on to the ferry across the Channel (no Eurostar in those days!) and another train to Paris Gare du Nord. From Paris on into Switzerland and the pretty town of Lausanne, where we had, in fact, booked a campsite. Then on into the glories of Italy and a highlight of the trip - spectacular Venice!

That was followed by quite a long train journey, through the slightly flimsier outer layer of the Iron Curtain to (then) Yugoslavia, and its mysterious capital Belgrade. From there another long night train journey down into Greece to historic Athens.

A detour from Athens was then planned, via its ancient port of Piraeus, to visit a number of, at that point unspecified, Greek islands of the Saronic group, before returning to the classical sights of the Greek capital.

Then we got inventive. Fiona had identified a cheap Russian shipping line, which offered a cross between a ferry and a cruise between Piraeus and Alexandria, in Egypt, via Larnaca in Cyprus and Latakia in Syria.

I managed to book our berths by repeatedly Telexing their headquarters in Odessa, from the Driving Test Booking Office in Edinburgh, where I was allegedly working at the time. Wonder if they ever found out.

The final stage to Cairo was to be by car, which would involve negotiating to hire a driver in Alexandria, who would take us a few hours by road to Egypt's capital. Might need my warm jumper.

What could possibly go wrong?

* * *

The point of telling you this tale of innocence and stupidity is not just to take yet another opportunity to relate one of our best-loved travel stories.

When I say "best-loved", I mean best-loved by the two of us. Not necessarily by our friends and family, who tend to now greet the words "Did we tell you about the time…?" with barely stifled groans and unkindly rolling eyes.

This trip in 1980 had a huge, mostly positive, effect on both of us. It laid the basis for holidays and travels over the next 40 years until Covid-19 came along and laid waste to our, and everyone else's, plans for 2020.

The 1980 trip to Cairo opened our eyes and our minds, to the influences of locations, climates, food, drink, people, history, archaeology - you get the idea. It made us resolve never to go back to Belgrade. It taught me not to take my t-shirt off at the Pyramids.

What I want to do in this book is to take that early basis and the lessons we knowingly or unknowingly absorbed, back then and through the subsequent years, and relate them to our much more recent travels.

I hope that by sharing our successes, our failures, and our downright disasters we might encourage other folk, at a time of our lives when we hopefully have significantly more time, and a bit more money, to keep believing that the world is our oyster and that we should just go and keep on experiencing it!

The term "silver surfer" makes me simultaneously feel slightly sick and causes me to develop a strong desire to punch the person who has used it.

One of Fiona's favourites is when we are in a restaurant in Edinburgh, late in the evening, and the young male waiter brings the bill.

"Off clubbing now, are we folks?" he remarks with a smirk. Because, of course, that would be unimaginable.

So original and undeniably hilarious. I genuinely really fear for what my wife will do the next time that happens, as it inevitably will.

CHAPTER 2: THE REST OF THAT TRIP

Edinburgh to Cairo: September - October 1980

Even at a distance of forty years, the prism of time leaves some things still sharp in the memory. Others have faded forever, probably to be only retrievable through hypnosis!

The abiding memories of a trip taken four decades ago form a general overall impression, punctuated by some pin-sharp recollections (landing in Latakia being one of them!). The whole gamut of experiences and recollections has been absorbed into the people we see ourselves as now.

The two twenty-somethings whom we were started out in Paris in September, and finished up in Cairo late in October. Between those two points, we felt that years of experiences had been crammed into seven weeks of our lives, some positive some not so positive.

In the intervening years, we've returned to some of the locations we visited - Paris, Lausanne, the Greek Islands (many times), and Egypt. Others left impressions that, whilst we may (or may not) have enjoyed them at the time, didn't produce a strong desire to return.

The Belgrade we visited in 1980 was not a city that has encouraged thoughts of a revisit. We arrived shortly after the death of Josip Broz (Tito), leader of the Partisans resistance movement in World War II, and President of the Socialist Federal Republic of Yugoslavia from 1953 until May 1980.

He had presided over a Yugoslavia which tried to encompass a range of disparate elements in a region in which conflict was no stranger, forming a country that was the most "westernised" of the Soviet Bloc and reputedly the least oppressive to live in.

The city we found was nervous about the future, in the wake of their unifier's passing. Living standards for many appeared to be low. In later years, we visited much poorer countries - India being a prime example. But in none of these countries were the people so rude, boorish, and unfriendly as those we encountered in the Serbian capital.

One clear memory was when Fiona jumped at the chance to spend an afternoon at the Red Star Belgrade football stadium, to get out of the city itself. This was unusual behaviour for her. On the way out to the stadium by local bus, she must have inadvertently sat in a seat reserved for the elderly or infirm.

At one stop, a very large local woman with impressive facial hair appeared through the entrance door and made a beeline for Fiona, all the time screaming (mercifully unintelligible) invective in her direction. Fiona made to get up, but the woman unceremoniously plonked her significant bulk in my girlfriend's lap, pinning her to the seat.

What began as an apology turned into some retaliatory yelling, until Fiona finally extricated herself, just in time to alight to enjoy the attractions of a vast and empty football stadium.

We sat in the top row of one side of the famous Red Star Stadium and drew our breath until we relaxed sufficiently to take some photos. The only other occupants were six small boys, who had climbed over the boundary wall, and were playing an enthusiastic game of three-a-side on the hallowed turf. Not a bad game, though I can't remember the final score.

Other friends had a very different experience of Belgrade, around the same time, so perhaps we were just unlucky. I'm sure things will have changed for the positive in modern times.

We spent one night in a cheap hotel beside Athens railway station when we were both laid low by colds. It was a typical, seedy railway station hotel, and our introduction to the Greek habit of putting used toilet paper in open waste baskets in the loo.

This depressing scenario made the decision for us to head to Piraeus, on the beautiful old wooden metro, to hop on a ferry to the nearest island chain, the Argo-Saronics.

The island chain consists of four better-known islands - Aegina, Poros, Hydra, and Spetses, plus a couple of less well-known ones. We decided to head out to Spetses first. On the way, the ferry drew into the harbour at Hydra, which we thought looked lovely. A fellow Brit leaning against the rail informed us that it was "Boring. Nothing on it," so we decided to give it a miss on the strength of his opinion.

Probably a big mistake - Hydra, like Verona, is now on our list of places we stupidly missed out on during that trip, which we still really want to visit. It did however teach us not to pay too much attention to other people's opinions. Everyone has their own tastes and preferences, which don't necessarily match ours.

Spetses, our first Greek island, was a revelation, a feeling reinforced by stopping off for a couple of nights on Poros and Aegina, on our way back to Athens. We fell completely in love with the dry heat, the magical quality of the Greek light, the blue Mediterranean, and the local dishes and wines - what we could afford, at any rate. Living was cheap, but our budget was tight!

Many a visit to other Greek island groups was to feature in our future trips, but you always remember your first time, and it was marvellous!

Athens was then, and probably still is, a city crammed full of wonderful things to see. Our first sight of the Acropolis was magical.

That particular visit turned comical when an American tourist asked me to take his photo with the famed temple as a backdrop. He said he would briefly move out of the shade and asked me to snap his photo as quickly as possible. It turned out that he feared that his new plastic knees would begin to melt in the hot Greek sun. It was hot, but not quite that hot!

The modern city was then crammed with cars, heavily polluted, and difficult to get about. As a modern metropolis, Athens was not that attractive, but its antiquities were well worth the small hardships.

From Piraeus, we hopped on our Black Sea shipping lines "cruise" to Alexandria, via Larnaca in Cyprus, and the aforementioned Latakia, on the coast of Syria.

It's worth remembering that we were on a Russian vessel in the time of the USSR. The cold war was still well in place. The staff on the boat were friendly but the food was fairly dire.

The most fascinating feature, however, was the ship's library. It was the duty of all good communists at the time to try to influence the thinking of visitors from the capitalist West. The library clearly reflected this, as the English language section held almost exclusively political tomes - Engels on Marx, and the like. I got two pages into one of those volumes and promptly gave up in favour of watching the waves go by.

The only two novels we could find in English were John Steinbeck's "The Grapes of Wrath" and John Galsworthy's "The Forsyte Saga."

The former told tales around the banking collapse and the Great Depression in the USA, at the end of the 1920s. Its main themes highlighted the evils of capitalism and its institutions.

"The Forsyte Saga" pointed up the ridiculous nature of the British class system between the world wars. I read both during the trip, and the less than subtle indoctrination kind of worked. Maybe I was at an impressionable age.

Larnaca in Cyprus was a brief, but attractive, stop-off, and Latakia has already been mentioned. I remember little of Alexandria, as we immediately negotiated a driver and car to take us to Cairo before it got too late in the day.

The road trip was quite long and uncomfortable. As darkness fell, it became obvious we would arrive in the huge metropolis of Egypt's capital city well after nightfall.

Not least because the car broke down in the dead of night in the middle of nowhere. Goats loomed up and peered in the windows at the strange alien invaders. We tramped back up the road to a large café, exclusively inhabited by local men, who were all watching the football on TV. So at least the evening wasn't a total write-off.

After some miraculous auto repairs, we asked to be dropped off in Cairo city centre. We were deposited at a tower block hotel, which presumably had some sort of arrangement with the driver. Something like 19 floors up in the Everest Hotel, we were shown to a room that had all the facilities listed outside. Among these was a porcelain wash hand basin. As a corner had been broken off, it didn't hold any water. We were too tired to argue, and we crawled between the none-too-white sheets and conked out.

Descending from our room to the lobby next morning was an exhilarating experience. The lift accelerated downwards from our floor, its speed increasing until it hit floor 13, appropriately enough, at which point some kind of arrest mechanism twanged into effect. This braking mechanism caused the elevator to jolt violently, but slow to a more sedate pace, to facilitate its safe arrival at the ground floor level. You got used to it after a while.

At that age, one's resilience is remarkable, or at least it seems so to our older selves now. Cairo proved to be a huge and difficult city to navigate. Even getting on a bus was a major challenge, as half of the bus "queue" alighted by the front steps, whilst the other half launched themselves aboard through the open windows.

Encountering some Egyptian men, whilst accompanied by a young blonde woman, was also educational. We never really adjusted to the feeling of discomfort, and what we interpreted as intimidation, as we walked about Cairo's streets.

We splashed out on a better hotel and, amongst other wondrous sights, eventually made it to the Pyramids at Giza! We again hired a driver and car to take us out to Giza - this time a young student at Cairo University. He had an unfortunate bump with another car on the way out to Giza, which may have been an omen for the rest of that day's trip.

We duly saw and entered the massive ancient structures, whilst declining an invitation to climb the outside of the Great Pyramid. But the overriding memory was of how stressful the visit was. We dispensed with our middle-aged Giza guide when it became apparent he couldn't stop hawking and spitting copiously into the sand, and was equally unable to unclamp his eyes from Fiona's chest. So, probably unadvisedly, we proceeded to find our own way about.

We got into an argument with a drinks seller at the foot of the Great Pyramid, who had sold us two bottles of what purported to be Pepsi Cola but tasted nothing like it. We harangued him for so long, that he actually gave us back the tiny amount of money we had paid him. It was the principle that counted!

Being a young Scottish male, the first thing you do when you get too hot in the midday sun is to take your top off. Naturally. This displays your puny, milky white body to all and sundry. The immediate effect on the plateau by the Pyramids was for a group of local youths to start shouting insults at us whilst mimicking apes dancing. Obviously baring one's torso was not the done thing, so it was my mistake.

Again unadvisedly, we felt moved to respond in kind, despite the fact that there were six or seven of them. Suddenly our driver screeched the car onto the Giza plateau, flung the door open, and yelled "Get in now!!"

We complied and were whisked away from our one and only ever (so far) visit to the Pyramids at Giza as if making our getaway from a bungled attempt at a bank robbery. We received a sound, and admittedly quite justified, telling off for my inappropriate behaviour, and we skulked back into Cairo in a bit of a huff.

Cairo was vast, oppressively over-populated, very hot, and exhausting. The air seemed to be the colour of sand, and to contain a fine suspension of an airborne desert so that everything had a brownish-yellow tinge. Our stomachs surprisingly survived eating a lunch of barbecued meat and pitta bread from a "clean" green plastic street stall plate. The method of cleaning was to wipe a previous customer's plate with a grimy rag before serving one's lunch on it.

At one point we were naïve enough to allow ourselves to be coaxed into an essence (perfume) shop as we walked by. The prosperous-looking owner first showed us photos of his prized assets: his large house, his large silver Mercedes car, and his slim blonde German wife. The pictures were all inserted under the glass surface of the main serving counter, so the customer could hardly fail to see them.

Around half an hour of hard sell followed until the proprietor realised that we genuinely didn't have much money, so were unlikely to be parted from it. In the end, honour was satisfied by us purchasing a small bottle of essence for the equivalent of £5 - our daily budget, you may remember.

We left the emporium and its (by now slightly grumpy) owner. We proceeded to argue about whose fault it was that we had stupidly allowed ourselves to be taken in, literally and metaphorically. Voices were raised and I turned towards Fiona to continue my half of the tirade.

This meant that I failed to see the aged, rust-encrusted cantilevered canopy in front of one of the shops we were passing. I promptly walked straight into it and split my head open.

Fiona was immediately concerned as the blood started running down my forehead from the resultant scalp would. Though I was sure I could detect a barely discernible smirk under her sympathetic demeanour. At least people gave us a wide berth on the pavement for a while.

The flight back to London, via Sofia and Brussels, meant a drop in temperature from 98 to -4 degrees F, so we knew we were home. We got off the train at Waverley Station with less than a pound Sterling left between us.

In hindsight, we were ill-prepared mentally for the trials of life without much spending money on the streets of Cairo. I remember clearly the feeling of relief when we came home, being able to walk about the centre of Edinburgh unmolested by passers-by.

The dragging, skin-chafing weight of the rucksack on my shoulders for six weeks or so is a feeling I can still effortlessly conjure up.

CHAPTER 3: EDINBURGH TO MAHÓN

September - October 2018

And so it came to pass that my career flashed past me. When I started my job in 1982, my 65th birthday in 2020 seemed impossibly far away. But we got older, our children grew up, and the time disappeared. Happily, punctuated by lots of enjoyable holidays along the way.

We reached a decision that I would retire at the age of 63, and so I duly did, at the end of June 2018. Fiona, being a few years younger, would continue to build up her internet business.

The majority of items that she retails reach the customer via drop-shipping direct from the supplier, so her business model lends itself to operating from virtually anywhere with a wi-fi signal, or the ability to use her mobile phone as a local hot spot. We have to admit that it is very satisfying to be sitting on a cliff top in the Spanish sunshine when an order drops into her inbox!

For some months before my retirement date, we were planning our first long trip. That really means that she was researching lots of places, modes of transport, apartments, and small hotels (definitely no tents).

Train travel appealed for a number of reasons, some altruistic, some selfish. Although we are not slavishly wedded to it, cutting down on the number of flights one takes is obviously desirable, given current climate change predictions. So we can feel a little better about travelling for six or seven weeks if minimal air travel is involved.

Eliminating the time spent hanging around airports is also a big plus. Fiona positively enjoys air travel, I do less so. So, taking all that stuff out of the equation is an overall positive benefit.

My own feelings on this subject may have been influenced by a trip I made with Fiona's brother Brian back in 1989 to Brussels, to watch our football team (Hibernian) play against the (now defunct) FC Liege in the latter city, in the EUFA Cup. The first leg in Edinburgh had been a nil-nil draw, so there was still everything to play for.

We bought cheap flights on an airline named Scottish European Airways (SEA). On the trip out to Brussels, we had to shout above the unusually loud engine noise in order to communicate with each other.

On our first night in Brussels, we kept apart from the main body of travelling supporters, dined well in the Toone district behind the Grand Place, and accidentally ambled back to our hotel through the red light district.

Very fortuitously, as it turned out, we got lost as we approached our hotel and missed the arcade which provided the quickest route to the hotel entrance. After a circuitous loop back we arrived safely, to find that fans walking through the arcade a little earlier had been attacked by youths wielding baseball bats.

By the time we got up to our room, the hotel bar was under sicge by youths brandishing poles and other implements, a scene which only subsided due to the arrival of a large contingent of riot police.

The next day, dumped in a rainy Liege hours before the kick-off, there was little to do but imbibe more Belgian beer and sample the delicious double-fried chips on offer.

The second leg went to extra time, and Hibs were finally beaten by a forty-yard wonder strike, which hit the net so hard that our goalie thought the shot had actually hit the crossbar. He tried to play on until he realised that he was the only one doing so.

As we walked across the tarmac to fly home the next day, people were jokingly taking bets on how far the plane would get, such was the scorched and decrepit appearance of the fuselage.

During the safety talk, the microphone failed. As we took off from the runway, all the lights down one side of the plane sparked out. Less than an hour into the flight, the propeller on the port engine distressingly ground to a halt, and the aircraft (if such a term could accurately be applied) tilted at an alarming angle.

The solitary flight attendant did a fantastic job of calming worried passengers down, telling us that the plane was designed to be able to fly on one engine. The flight was full, occupied only by Hibs supporters, plus a Belgian couple who had won a trip to Edinburgh in a competition. Unfortunately, the Belgian lady in question was wearing an uncomfortable-looking neck brace, as she had recently been in a car crash. Lucky white heather.

Those who were actually awake gradually managed to settle down as we progressed toward home, albeit canted at a strange angle to the horizontal. Relative silence reigned until suddenly a previously unseen chap, wearing an oil-stained maroon jumper and carrying a quite large piece of metal of unidentified origin, walked quickly up the aisle from the back of the plane and into the cockpit.

There was a stunned silence as everyone looked at everyone else with the same unspoken thought: "I hope that's not a bit we need to stay in the air??!!"

Eventually, we limped into Norwich to make an emergency landing, speeding along the runway pursued by fire engines and other emergency vehicles. When we had disembarked and were waiting to board another propeller-driven plane (gulp) to finally get back up to Edinburgh, I spotted the pilot sitting alone in the otherwise empty cafeteria.

I went over to thank him for his skill in getting us down safely. By way of conversation. I suggested that he was no doubt experienced in such events and it was all in a day's work for him. He raised his ashen face and said flatly:

"Never done anything like that before mate."

I think travelling by train also takes us both back to exciting trips away from home when we were children. Hardly anyone we knew flew in those days, and my family never owned a car, so trains were the main form of longer-distance transport for us then.

Although the statistics would tell us otherwise, the train seems instinctively to feel a safer way to go than an aeroplane (especially if you ever flew with Scottish European Airways). It's on the ground the whole time, and you can watch the world go by, whilst being lulled into a pleasantly soporific stupor by the countryside flashing by, to the soundtrack of the rhythmic sounds of the train's passage between stations.

When you arrive at your destination, you don't have to negotiate the long trip into the city from an outlying airport in an often exorbitantly expensive taxi. And the uncomfortable feeling that you may have "*I've just landed in this strange place. Please rip me off,*" tattooed on your forehead, as you approach the taxi rank.

Whilst we both lack the capacity for delving into the detailed minutiae beloved of real train enthusiasts, it is a bonus to be surprised by the range and variety of rolling stock you encounter in the course of a series of train journeys. Sometimes very surprised.

For us, the enjoyment of travelling around by train is two-fold. One, to enjoy the actual experience of our favourite form of passenger locomotion, in as relaxed a manner as possible. Two, to arrive in new, or old favourite, locations and to stay long enough to get to know them at least passably well. The whistle-stop tour, arriving in the evening and leaving the next day, in order to tick off a visit on the list, isn't the motivation for us.

The length of stay in any one location is obviously a compromise, which encompasses what we want to see and do in any given place, how many places we want to see on a given trip, and how much ground we have to cover in the allotted time, and of course our budget! I tend to want to squeeze in more stops, then regret having to move on more quickly than becomes desirable.

The bulk of planning of all our travels falls to Fiona, because (a) she's very good at it, and (b) she actually does enjoy it. So months of research ensued, with me being consulted at strategic moments. We arrived at an itinerary. As I always do, I tried to squeeze a couple more places in along the way, and ultimately settled for one.

In common with our 1980 trip, we decided upon the list and order of places we were going to visit. Unlike in 1980, this time we did have an itinerary to which we had to stick, as we booked all of our accommodation and as much of our transport as we could, in advance of us setting off.

The reasons for this were mainly three-fold. One, we were almost 40 years older, and we didn't want the hassle of looking for accommodation as we went along. Secondly, this also allowed for careful selection of interesting and conveniently situated places to stay, which was the subject of much discussion and debate. Vrbo, Airbnb, and Hotels.com weren't around in 1980.

Last but not least, we had the comfort of knowing that (at least in theory) most of our train and all of our plane journeys were booked in advance, saving the time which would inevitably be spent milling around train and bus stations.

We still have friends who prefer to hire a car, even in places we'd be hesitant about driving in, and to look for suitable accommodation as they go along. It has always seemed to us that the double whammy of spending lots of time trying to find somewhere good to stay, instead of chilling at the location and quite possibly ending up in an area that is less than ideal, argues against this approach. Still, everyone to their own.

The feeling of being more spontaneous and acting off the cuff presumably makes that approach to things preferable for some other folk. If our travels together have taught us anything about ourselves, it's that situations like that tend to cause us to fall out big style, which is best avoided in the interests of preserving harmony in the wider universe.

Equally, we have also learned that it's best not to try to influence even the closest of friends to do things the way we would do them.

A prime, and very unfortunate, example is a very good female friend whose marriage had ended messily. She was unsure what path to take for some time afterward, and we encouraged her to travel whilst she took the time to equilibrate and arrive at a plan for her future.

We even gave her an inspirational autobiography, written by a young woman in a similar situation, who hailed from Dundee. This adventurous Dundonian lady travelled across North African deserts, always with a black cocktail dress rolled up in her backpack. For a while, she became the quasi-wife of a *Tuareg* chief, living in tented communities beside oases and travelling by camel.

After a year of us badgering her, our friend decided on something slightly less exotic. She answered an advert to crew a yacht (her former husband and she had been keen sailors) from Southampton to the Caribbean. On arrival, the yacht was to be raced whilst she treated herself to a lovely three-week holiday in the sun.

At the same time, we were on a short holiday in Greece. When we arrived back at Gatwick airport, the newspaper racks of tabloids had our friend's photo emblazoned over a front-page story. The headline read "BRITISH HEIRESS IN DRAMATIC HELICOPTER RESCUE!" We sat down in the airport to read the sorry tale.

On its way to the sun-drenched Caribbean, the yacht had only made it as far as the Bay of Biscay, where it was caught in a fierce storm, a bad one even for that neck of the woods. Our poor friend ended up praying on her knees on the deck as she waited to be winched up to a rescue helicopter. She was in the queue after the yacht's captain, who gallantly was the first one off his sinking ship.

After the successful rescue, she was taken to spend the night at a seaman's mission on the coast of Galicia.

When reports of the yacht rescue incident reached the UK, the tabloids had randomly put together her first and middle names with her ex-husband's surname, had added a hyphen, and had decided that she was a double-barrelled heiress of some note, from a family of landed gentry in England.

The red tops had sought confirmation of that from her supposed parents. They had told the newspapers that it was definitely *not* the case. The tabloid press had gone ahead and printed it as fact anyway.

So, as you can imagine, she never listened to any advice from us ever again. But I digress.

The plan for my retirement trip number one was to fly from Edinburgh to Porto, stay for a few days, then catch the famous train along the Douro valley, almost to the end of the impossibly picturesque line, and the barrio called *Bairro do Casal* in the village of Murça, for a slightly longer stay. Then back to Porto and head south to the ancient University town of Coimbra. On to the Portuguese border town of Guarda to catch the bus into Spain and visit spectacular Salamanca.

On again to my inserted extra stopover - the ancient walled city of Avila. Train again from Avila to Madrid, then the high-speed AVE to Sevilla.

After a few days in sweltering Sevilla another train trip to the lesser-known El Puerto de Santa Maria, the port servicing the bodegas of the sherry triangle of San Lucar, Jerez de la Frontera, and El Puerto de Santa Maria itself, by giving access to the huge port of Cádiz at Spain's southwestern tip.

From El Puerto de Santa Maria, a day visit to Jerez, before boarding just the second plane of the trip to Palma de Mallorca, for a couple of nights. From Palma, an early morning Trasmediterranea ferry to Mahón, on the white and blue island of Menorca.

Planning for my retirement in June 2018 included a lot of planning for this first post-retirement trip, leaving in September.

As I mentioned earlier, most of the planning is done by Fiona as it is definitely her forte. I am brought in to help decide between possible flats, apartments, and small hotels for us to stay in along the way. And to be discouraged from trying to fit in too many stops.

One thing we learned whilst doing longer trips when we are older is that it's definitely better for us to spend a little more time in some locations. Moving on every couple of days seemed fine when we were younger, but it's less appealing in practice nowadays.

Having your accommodation booked in advance does make the itinerary more rigid and does inevitably remove some of the scope for spontaneity and divergence from the plan.

On the upside, however, it gives the reassurance of knowing where you will be spending the night (assuming you don't get on the wrong train) and saves countless hours looking for a place as you go. This is particularly important if you are quite fussy, sorry discerning, about the accommodation you stay in.

Booking as much of your train and other travel before you go also provides reassurance. Booking seats in advance gives you a specific coach to aim for, although some awkward discussion may ensue if someone is erroneously occupying your seats. Or if you get on the wrong coach and have to annoy everyone else by dragging suitcases through a crowded train - one of our specialties.

It also saves a lot of time. One leg we couldn't book from home was the hugely picturesque train trip from Porto along the side of the Douro valley to Murça. It took us about an hour in Porto railway station to decipher the wall-mounted timetables and seek guidance from the information point, before we were sure we'd bought tickets for the right train on the right day. Porto's Sao Bento, however, turns out to be a very attractive place to hang out, as railway stations go.

CHAPTER 4: EDINBURGH

After all the discussion and planning, we are on our way! You would think that getting from our house to Edinburgh Airport, and onto a flight to Porto, would be relatively straightforward.

All is well as we leave on time to pick up our daughter Kathleen and her partner Lewis - Kathleen is taking custody of our car after dropping us off at the airport.

As Fiona drives us westwards, I have the temerity to ask: "Are you sure you are in the correct lane, dear?" to turn right along the Queensferry Road.

"Yes!" I am tersely assured. "Do you think I'm going to get lost on the way to Edinburgh Airport?"

So I hold my tongue a few moments later when she drives past the turn-off at Barnton, and heads for the Forth Road Bridge. There are no further turns off after that, so we do a lovely tour with a view of the bridges, and a clear vista of the Fife coast, before we double back and eventually get to Edinburgh airport.

This slight kink in proceedings does, however, serve to acquaint Lewis, who is sitting very quietly in the back wishing he'd decided to do something else with his afternoon, with the calm and reasonable way our family tends to interact in increasingly tense situations.

Having managed to negotiate our lunch at the airport without actually choking, we make our way to the appointed Gate for our flight. Just as we should be boarding, the Gate sign changes from

"Porto" to "Palma", and a whole new planeload of eager people descend on the Gate.

At this point, things all become the fault of a friend, or rather of her mother and father, for having conceived her on the particular day that they did. As we sit at the Gate, I've been trying to wish her a happy birthday on Facebook, but I can't access wi-fi or 4G on my mobile. I'm midway through using Fiona's phone to do it when the aforementioned Gate change happens.

We spring up and head for the Departures screens to locate our new Gate. I've just fought my way through the oncoming tide of stressed passengers when I realise with that sinking feeling of instant panic that I don't have my phone.

I push back into the milling mass of people surrounding the Gate, yelling "Has anyone found an iPhone?" A number of very helpful folk respond that a man has picked it up.

One very nice lady points at a sheepish-looking gentleman and shouts "He has it!". More information rapidly follows, and I am joyfully reunited with my precious phone at the Gate desk. Losing that would have been a good start.

Meanwhile, Fiona has discovered that, far from having lost something, she has something in her possession that she shouldn't. She has in her pocket one of our two car keys, which was meant to be left with Kathleen as a spare, so Kathleen better not lose the one she has. Texts and phone calls follow to ensure that the daughter knows she is in possession of the one and only key she's going to get for the next six weeks or so.

By now, we feel like two elderly people, perhaps travelling abroad for the first time, sadly confused by our own incompetence.

At least the flight is good. Contrary to many stories Ryanair's staff are very nice. We are delivered to our flat in Porto, at the promised cost, by a very friendly taxi driver.

CHAPTER 5: PORTO AND AVEIRO

Our taxi ride into the city from Porto's Francisco Sa Carneiro airport takes us through a cross-section of the city's districts. As we approach our destination, the Air BnB flat we chose all those months ago back in Edinburgh, the streets become narrower. The buildings appear more run down and the general ambience is more rough and ready.

Spray painting seems to be a popular pastime. The genre in our district looks more like gang and political slogans to me, as opposed to urban artistic expression. Still, there's a handy supermarket fifty metres away from our front door. And a few down-at-heel-looking bars further up the street.

We alight from the taxi.

"I think we could say that the neighbourhood is up-and-coming," suggests Fiona, taking an initial look up and down the street outside our apartment block. Looks to me like it hasn't come up very far, from quite a low plateau.

However, our Air BnB apartment is secure, compact, and handily situated. Space is limited, but a lot of thought has gone into maximising its efficient use. When we travel for this length of time, it's not financially sensible, nor probably desirable, to eat out every evening.

Mixing in some self-catering is economically sound and it also ensures variety when we feel like it. The local supermarket turns out to be crammed with provisions and is reasonably priced. Remarkably nice Portuguese wine always seems to be available at a few Euros a bottle.

Our table outside the small local Venezuelan bar wobbles on the aged black and white cobbles covering the street. The evening is balmy and the atmosphere is relaxed. The waitress is faintly reminiscent of Shakira (who is Colombian, I know). This is a good start.

Six weeks of travelling lie before us and the prospect is inviting! Also lying before us is my first beer (Venezuelan *Zulia*) of the trip and Fiona's glass of generously poured red wine. Formal measures seem to be just a regrettable error of judgment practiced in Scotland.

We are both excited by the prospect of the trip, but we each know that the other is apprehensive too. It's a long time since we have been away from home for so long. The separation from our children, albeit they are no longer kids, will be the longest since they were born. On the plus side, we now have mobile phones, Skype, and so on, none of which were available thirty-eight years ago.

"Do you reckon we'll stay the course OK?" asks Fiona. Chatting over our drinks, she is the first to broach the subject of our ability to enjoy this long period of travelling. We are considerably longer in the tooth, though having a little more money, and the advent of Air BnB and Hotels.com, should ensure that our creature comforts are better catered for than in the past.

"We're also going to be in each other's company 24/7. Will I get through it without wanting to kill you?" she muses. Surely in our relative dotage, we'll be able to get along with fewer fallings-out than during the Cairo trip. That was in our younger, more fiery days. Or am I being overly optimistic?

"Well, we're about to find out!" I respond helpfully. "I guess the folks who run this nice wee bar probably have a lot more to be apprehensive about than we do." Venezuela has been very much in the news lately, with its collapsing economy accompanied by civil unrest. We suspect that the bar owners will have loved ones back home, and underneath their cheery exterior will lie concern for their family and friends.

We are on the edge of Porto's University district, in an area that has obviously been decaying for some time, but which is now being upgraded. Sitting outside on the cobbled street affords us the first opportunity to watch the local people go by.

The shiny black and white cobbled area at first looks as though it will be a pedestrian precinct, but people of all ages, dogs, motorbikes, bicycles, cars, vans, and lorries all seem to co-exist in relative peace and harmony.

Groups of bright young University students are strolling along between bars, laughing and flirting, as is to be expected.

"Looks like not a bad place to come to University, if you were a young chap who had the opportunity," I observe innocently.

Following my gaze, Fiona responds "Shut up, you old pervert," most unnecessarily, I feel. I was actually referring to the general ambience, not just the frequent groups of attractive young students strolling by.

Every now and then, a face appears in the crowd which indicates that it's not just happy young students who frequent this district. One or two seriously heavy-looking dudes wander past. They are sporting disturbing facial tattoos and have very discouraging auras.

This automatically makes me feel a little tense. I also have a terrible habit of continually glancing at someone who looks menacing. This is not a wise policy. However, everyone seems to be rubbing along amicably, and the atmosphere remains relaxed and enjoyable.

We've noticed on previous visits to Portuguese cities, Lisbon is a perfect example, that they can be quite edgy, especially after dark. Upmarket districts and people seem to mingle cheek by jowl with poverty and dodgy-looking characters. As poorer districts become gentrified, this mix inevitably intensifies. From this evening's limited observations, Porto seems to be another example.

The next day, we take one of the beautiful old trams (Number 18 with *Massarelos* on the front) part of the way downhill to the near end of the impressive Ponte de Dom Luis I - the bridge over the Douro into the Vila Nova de Gaia district. We set out across the bridge's expanse in glorious sunshine.

"Don't step back!" shouts Fiona, as I try to position myself to photograph the best possible views across to both sides of the Douro, and down onto the Ribera district by the waterside. Today, Porto is spectacularly photogenic in the hot sun.

It does feel a little unsettling to have a very quiet, albeit slow-moving, train/metro running along the centre of this bridge in both directions, with no barriers between pedestrians and the track.

Porto is quite a compact and walkable city, as long as you don't mind hills. When we reach the far end of the Ponte de Dom Luis I, we start to wind our way downhill towards the tightly packed buildings, which gradually rise up the next hill.

Vila Nova de Gaia houses the traditional port wine lodges for which the city is famous. The only problem is that Porto, like every other city in Portugal, seems to have been built on the sides of a series of very steep hills. When you go down, you have to come back up, which becomes tiring and thirsty work in the ambient temperatures.

We walk around the confusingly winding streets in the heat, trying to find the world-renowned Taylor's Port wine lodge, where we've booked a tour. I lose count of the number of times we walk uphill, then downhill again, then gradually swing round on a more gently climbing curve. Clearly, we don't have as good a sense of where the lodge is as we thought we did, and equally clearly, we're not taking the most direct route. If indeed such a thing exists.

By now we are both very hot, quite sweaty, and a tad irritable. Normal practice in these circumstances would be for us to start to bicker somewhat, but we manage to refrain. I am accused of exhibiting my customary poor sense of direction, but that is such a given that I can't really offer any arguments in mitigation.

Eventually, we trace a roundabout route to the lodge's impressive front entrance gate, which is set in a searingly white wall. We arrive hot, perspiring, and bedraggled. We grab a seat in Taylor's lovely rose garden, with the intention of re-hydrating before our tour.

"Can I have a beer please?" No, sorry, we don't serve beer. "Coke?" Sorry, no. We only serve the products of Taylor's Lodge - a wide variety of ports and grape juice, and still water.
Water it is then. I get the purist approach, but on hot days like this, they really are missing a trick!

The British connection in Vila Nova de Gaia is obvious and strong. The port-wine lodge route includes Churchill's, Croft, and Graham's, as well as Taylor's of Fladgate.

We had decided on a visit to Taylor's out of the range of available wine lodges because we like the idea that it has remained an independent family business since its foundation in 1692. Also, the lodge tour is self-guided - we much prefer going at our own chosen pace, rather than that of a substantial group of people. The tour is excellent.

"Look at the size of this place!" enthuses Fiona, as we make our way through the corridors between hundreds of barrels in the vast, high-roofed main hall.

The comfortingly musty aroma of fermenting alcohol provides a constant olfactory backdrop, which will no doubt become very familiar as our trip progresses through Portugal and Spain. The general sense of timelessness, and the connection with specific practices which have endured through multiple generations, is very alluring.

After visiting the informative museum section of the wine lodge, we return happily to the lovely rose garden at the tour's conclusion, to taste a range of excellent Port wines of various hues. The white "Chip Dry" is a particular favourite.

There is more than a hint of an English country garden in the air. Birds twitter agreeably. A mild breeze adds to our feelings of comfort. Muted conversations and appreciative noises reach us from the other, well-spaced tables. The environment is perfect for enjoying the experience of sampling Taylor's finest products, which we do at our leisure.

We decide to catch a river taxi back across the Douro to Cais de Estiva on the Ribera side. The design of these *rabellas* is inspired by the traditional boats that were used to transport Port wine from the vineyards of the Douro Valley into the cellars of Vila Nova de Gaia's lodges.

The boat master's uniform also reflects that worn by the crews of the *rabello* boats of bygone days. Under his command, the trip leaves frequently (every 15 minutes), is quick (around 5 minutes), and cheap (around 3 Euros). Too short actually, as the crossing affords highly photogenic views of the Douro bridges and Ribera itself as we approach it.

Another day, we approach the Ribera district from up the hill on the Porto side, again taking a beautiful old wooden Number 18 tram from the square beside the Igreja das Carmelitas - a huge church, its external walls decorated with stunning sky blue and white tiles.

Apparently, there used to be a law in Portugal that no two churches could share the same wall. In this case, rumour has it that this was essential to discourage amorous liaisons between the nuns of the Carmelitas church and the monks of the adjacent Igreja do Carmo. So, what may be Portugal's narrowest house - about one metre wide - was built between the two neighbouring churches.

This micro house was apparently occupied until the 1980s. You'd think that perhaps the owner could have made a bit of extra income by renting his bedroom out to the.... nah, perhaps better not go there. Maybe he wouldn't have wanted to be seen to be encouraging bad habits.

When we alight from the tram, we start to walk downhill towards the river. We are confronted with a building that seems almost emblematic of Porto at this exact point in time. It's five stories high and appears to be pretty much just a façade. Every window is an empty eye socket, some bearing the signs of fire and smoke having flashed out onto the building's stone frontage.

On level four, the fine wrought-iron balconies are preserved, miraculously intact. At street level, Porto's urban artists have taken over, with nicely executed images of green aliens, a cartoon cow, and a cannibal with his boiling caldron, amongst others.

However, regeneration is underway. As this, and countless other, buildings in Porto make their transition from near ruin to a refurbished apartment block, they pass through an interim phase of their lives as vibrantly colourful street art canvases.

As we wind on down the hill towards Ribera, the area is very attractive. The restaurants do become generally more expensive as you get closer to the waterside, and it is very busy. Once on the quayside, we are approached by some sweet young ladies, whose heavy-looking black cloaks seem at odds with the ambient temperature.

"Would you like to make a donation to our local University?" one asks, very politely. I don't know whether this is an unusual con trick played on unsuspecting tourists or a genuine thing. I mumble something about donating to a University back home in Scotland, and to one in Colorado, and politely decline.

The young ladies melt into the crowds in search of better pickings, looking only slightly disappointed. More of the black cloaks when we get to Coimbra.

A sightseeing boat trip, from the Ribera quayside, takes us onto the Douro river. The pace is slow, and we have plenty of opportunities to appreciate the impressive series of bridges under which we glide. A scenic cable car plies back and forth above the Vila Nova de Gaia side. Porto seems huddled together and jammed with people, but vibrant and interesting, with something always going on in this liveliest of cities.

After our boat trip - always a good way to airily cool down on a day like this - we climb a flight of stairs to a small square. A radiant white bride and her smartly suited groom are dancing romantically to the playing of a lone violinist, in the slanting late afternoon sun. They seem oblivious to the small crowd of onlookers. They stop dancing to kiss, with her headdress billowing in the breeze blowing off the river. The world feels like a good place today.

The ancient trams still traverse the city and are a favourite, and airy, way to get your bearings. At the end of the Number One tram route (with *Passeio Alegre* on the front), out along the waterfront to Foz do Douro, we have to get out and walk the last few hundred metres, as someone has carelessly parked their bright red car too close to the tram track.

At least they haven't put their hazard lights on, to confirm that "Yes, I'm definitely causing an obstruction, and I know it." The tram driver's resigned look indicates that this is not an uncommon event.

Foz do Douro has a seaside-like feel to it. Hundreds of seagulls flock around the empty lobster creels by the water. A pleasantly cooler breeze is a welcome development. Helicopter rides can be taken from just along the waterfront.

We've mistimed the late afternoon closing time for the funicular railway back up from Ribera, so we enquire how much it would be for one of the assembled tuk-tuks to take us back up the steep hill. We try not to laugh at the price offered. In the end, Uber comes to the rescue.

The Harry Potter phenomenon kind of passed us by. Our children's primary school seemed to be obsessed with these tales of magic and mystery, even organising Sports Day on a Harry Potter theme. Our kids never really caught the bug and neither did we.

However, coming from JK Rowling's home town, we could hardly leave Porto without a visit to the Livraria Lello - reputed to be an amazing old bookshop, which the author allegedly frequented when she lived here.

With its beautifully carved stone frontage, enhanced by pastel colouring between the carvings, it is indeed a fantastic building architecturally and aesthetically. It is, however, also a complete sell-out to commercial greed.

We make two attempts to visit the hallowed premises, eventually queueing for ages in an unwelcome shower of warm rain to gain entry by paying 10 Euros. This entitles us to walk around the shop's interior. Hundreds of other visitors do the same, and so we all have the privilege of dodging each other, particularly the shoal of selfish selfie-takers on the quirky spiral staircases.

Our annoyance grows pricklier by the minute. I start deliberately not trying to avoid bumping into people. Which is childish and petulant. It's the proprietors, not the other visitors, who give rise to most of the disgruntlement.

The Livraria's whole display area seems fake - books for tourists, including split new-looking limited editions of English classics. All in all, we wish we hadn't bothered. We give up and flounce out in a snit.

As we wind our way downhill from the Livraria Lello, we pass a number of street entertainers. One bearded chap has long plaited fair hair. He wears a black beret and a very sad expression.

He sits behind a small wooden music machine, whose name I don't know, surrounded by books, a sinister plaster gnome, a hen, and a small boy with a cap, who looks like a character from a Charles Dickens novel. The whole scenario isn't exactly jolly.

Another sits on a small folding chair wearing a blue football top and a straw hat, desultorily playing his accordion. He is accompanied by a sad-looking little dog which is perched on an even smaller folding table. It may be sad due to the fact that it is wearing some sort of grey jacket with a spotted neckerchief and has a small purse dangling around its neck.

Moving on down the sweeping curved road towards the station, we arrive at Sao Bento railway station, walk in the main entrance, and are immediately entranced by the main hall. Sao Bento has to be one of the most attractive stations in the world.

It's worth a visit as a sight in its own right, even if you aren't about to travel by train. Passengers mill about looking confused but are intermittently captivated by the towering ornate ceiling and arched windows.

Most engaging of all are the 20,000 stunning painted tiles which adorn the walls. These predominantly blue and white tiles, by the artist Jorge Colacao, are called *azujelos*, and they vividly depict scenes from Portugal's history.

The station was built in 1900 on the site of a former convent, and it feels more like the ballroom of a stately home than it does a railway station.

The station is also the starting point for the famous *Linha do Douro*, the track which winds its way up the Douro Valley and back, alongside the meandering river. The reason we are here is that we need to buy our tickets for that journey, as we couldn't purchase them on the Web before we left home.

It takes us about an hour of milling about the busy station concourse to be certain we have correctly interpreted the timetables pinned to the wall outside the ticket office. We also have to queue to seek assistance from one of the ticket clerks.

Eventually, we are sure that we have booked the correct trains on the right days at the right times for our journey up the valley to Coa, and back in due course. It then takes a bit longer to queue up and actually purchase the tickets. Portuguese may look a bit like Spanish when written, but it sounds more like an Eastern European language to us. We get there in the end.

Porto has many fabulous, eminently photographable old buildings, a substantial number with spectacularly tiled exteriors. Many of these buildings are empty. However, there is an upward shift in the air, renovation work is everywhere, cranes proliferate, and both the tourism and construction businesses appear to be booming.

We unashamedly like places where we feel that we can eat and drink well and get good value for our money. Porto reminds us that Portugal tends to specialise in this aspect of living, and we're very happy that we've made it our first port of call.

A day trip from Porto takes us to Aveiro. The town is dubbed Portugal's Venice by some people who have overactive imaginations. I had originally wanted to spend a couple of days here but had been dissuaded on the grounds of trying to fit in too many stops. This turns out to be a good decision.

We arrive in Aveiro by train, to a city that immediately feels compact, clean, and a mix of the traditional and the modern. The railway station is a five-minute walk from the river bank, which is intermittently crossed by some pretty stone bridges. We decide to take a canal boat tour. Everyone else seems to be.

The sun is shining and the air is warm. It's always good to be on the water in the middle of a town or city. We chug contentedly along Aveiro's network of nice, modern-looking canals on which there are some attractively decorated bridges, bearing colourful coats of arms. The boatman's commentary drones on in the background.

Aveiro has its own answer to gondolas, in one of which we are currently perched. These long narrow *moliceiros* are former fishing boats that now provide access along the Ria for tourist trips. The resemblance to Venice ends there.

The bows of these vessels, for some reason, famously bear saucy painted images. Young ladies flashing their ample bosoms or young chaps looking up the girls' skirts. I use the word "saucy" because they remind me of the old, traditional seaside "rude" postcards that used to be on display on British promenades in my childhood, but without the clumsily suggestive verbal jokes.

"Not really all that racy, are they?" observes Fiona, tartly.

I can't seem to find any explanation as to why the boats are decorated in this way. They just are. Your maiden aunt would not be shocked by the prow art on these allegedly risqué vessels. Any self-respecting Venetian would choke on his Barolo at the comparison between the two cities.

As a town, we conclude that Aveiro is perfectly nice, in an inoffensive sort of way. It doesn't really seem to offer much else, so a day trip definitely suffices for us. Right again, Fiona.

Helpful Hints: Porto and Aveiro

Take comfortable footwear - you are likely to be walking a lot in Porto. Also always carry water. We wished we had when we visited Taylor's bodega.

Definitely head across the river to Vila Nova de Gaia. A tour of a port wine lodge is a standard tourist activity, but it's well worth the small trip.

Go on the River Douro, even for just a short boat ride. The views from both banks are beautiful.

If time allows, try the cable car on the Vila Nova de Gaia side, and the funicular on the Ribera side. We ran out of time for those. And there's always the helicopter!

Use the trams. They are wonderful.

Aveiro is not very like Venice, but it is a nice day trip if time allows. Your ten-year-old son/grandson may think that the boat murals are racy.

CHAPTER 6: MURÇA AND DOURO VALLEY

The Times *"Great Railway Journeys of the World"* by Julian Holland tells us that *"Home to the world-famous Port-wine industry, the highly scenic Douro Valley is served by a broad-gauge railway from Porto. Giving passengers breath-taking views of the river valley and its steep-sided vineyards, the railway carried international traffic to and from Spain until 1984, when the Spanish rail link was closed."*

"I can't see out the bloody windows!" I whine.

"I know, the spray paint comes about a third of the way up!" agrees Fiona, frustratedly.

The woman in the set of seats in front of us now rattles down her window blind, no doubt to block out the warm afternoon sun, and coincidentally our forward view through her window.

And so we commence what promises to be the most scenic and most enjoyable railway journey of our trip. The timetables and routings along the banks of the Douro can be slightly challenging. Some trains only go on some days. Some only stop at some stations. But basically, you can get a train up the valley and a train back down to Porto Sao Bento. You can watch the river boats from the train, or the train from the river boats.

We change seats a couple of times, to try to get a generally less interrupted view. We also hop across to the other side of the carriage from time to time, to be on the side of the train which offers the most beautiful scenery at that moment. The locals are obviously so used to the spectacular views that they seem to barely notice. A bit like us walking along Princes Street beneath Edinburgh Castle, I guess.

As our artistically re-decorated train winds gradually along the bank of the Douro, the sunny vistas become gradually more and more spectacular. Row upon row of vines clamber up the steep hillsides, and the river takes on an almost fjord-like quality.

We know that the temperature rises the further up the valley we progress and that the hottest areas in general, are best for Port wine production. Well-known wine producers have their own railway stations, servicing their vineyards and buildings.

Despite the visual impediments, the train ride is spectacular. It's also great to look forward to doing it all in reverse when you make the journey back.

But why, oh why, Portuguese Railways, don't you make the most of it for everyone travelling on your most famous and scenic line by putting some decent new rolling stock on the tracks, and keeping it (like other Portuguese trains) bright and clean?

By rail, as long as you get off at the correct station along the Douro line, you can't really go wrong. We manage to get it right, and we are picked up at the deserted Coa station by Anabela, the lady who owns the re-developed village homes in the Bairro do Casal area of Murça, with a population of circa 70, up the steep hill from the station.

"Welcome to Murça!" she smiles, genuinely proud of the impact the surroundings make on a first-time visitor. Her friendliness and concern for our comfort and enjoyment are to be a constant theme of our stay.

Anabela has patiently purchased modest village homes in Bairro do Casal, as locals have passed away or otherwise left, and she has refurbished these to a very high standard. Six or seven such homes, spread throughout the small area which constitutes Bairro do Casal, together make up her unique hotel.

Each home bears the name of the local family which formerly owned the property - ours is named "*Formosinda's House*". These

45

beautifully refurbished buildings cost only around 72 Euros per night, which we reckon is excellent value.

The district definitely looks like a one-horse kind of town. Going anywhere involves walking either uphill or downhill, with few level areas. Seeing another inhabitant is quite a notable event.

As we go about checking into our village house, with Anabela's assistant Aida, in a reception area that seems to have been hewn out of the local rock, we are greeted with glasses of the slightly elicit "Port wine that cannot say its name". Each year there are apparently quotas of Port wine made, after which no more of the product can be classified as "Port". This ruby red fortified wine comes from excess production, and it is fresh, fruity, and delicious.

Our home for the next week is a superbly refurbished village house, with a lovely reddish wooden veranda, in the upper village. The view over the vine-covered hillsides, from the side of the outdoor swimming pool down to the slow-flowing blue of the Douro, is endlessly spectacular. The heat this far up the valley, which helps provide the ideal temperatures for Port production, can be stifling.

On our first night there, we decide to have a drink on our little veranda before eating. It's still hot well after sundown, in September, and it's very dark indeed. The endless hum of cicadas provides soothing background music. but unfortunately, they have other insect friends to keep them company.

We beat a hasty and undignified retreat indoors when an unidentified insect the size of a fist lands beside us on the wall. An insect-discouraging candle is clearly no match for this monster. In fact, it probably devoured the candle. We never went back out to investigate.

Each evening we return to find that the next day's breakfast has been put in our fridge - fresh local produce, fruit, jams, and more. Still warm newly baked bread is left in a small bag hanging on our door to greet us when we rise each morning.

"Could get used to this..." observes Fiona happily.

We decide to try the in-house cooking for dinner, which Aida describes almost apologetically as simple, straightforward rural fare. It is so good that we never have dinner anywhere else. The wines provided are all local and all superb. I ask for a six-pack of Superbock beer and it arrives within ten minutes, perfectly chilled.

After dinner, it is very dark. There isn't really anywhere to go. The TV reception is patchy and not very interesting, and the wifi can be dodgy. So it's a good book and early to bed, with only the night sounds of the insects to keep us company.

When we get up in the morning, I open the shutters on the small window in the bedroom, which looks out over the valley. The mists rise languorously as the vines come alive with the touch of the rising sun. Another hot day is in prospect.

We soon realise that Anabela and Aida are the most hospitable hosts one could hope to encounter. Nothing is too much trouble for them. They run us to and from Coa railway station, to a restaurant, if we want to eat out, down to Canada do Inferno to see the rock carvings and the fantastic modern museum, and out to a small local *quinta* for a very boozy personal wine tour and tasting.

For our excursion to see the World Heritage site containing the famous Coa Valley prehistoric rock carvings, we assemble at an agreed meeting place to catch our jeep. This drops us above the favoured spot for viewing the carvings, together with our guide Marina, who is a local student. Our group includes two other older couples, as we clamber down into the Canada do Inferno. By the time we reach the side of the river, we are fully aware of why its name is Inferno!

The other couples are perhaps slightly older than us, but they are slimmer, fitter, and look like seasoned hikers. "I hope we can make it back up OK. Getting stuck would be really embarrassing," worries Fiona.

By now, I'm sweating heavily. Even though she's wearing a vest top and shorts Marina's brow is visibly perspiring, but she does it much more decorously.

She draws our attention to the fascinating carvings - rock art that dates back to Paleolithic times. The engravings were discovered during work to construct a dam in the Coa valley.

They consist of thousands of depictions of horses, cows, and other animals that the people of the time encountered, only a small number of which we could examine. With our guide's assistance we make out the different animals, and even marvel at what must be the earliest attempts at animation - a nodding horse's head cleverly carved into one of the stone slabs, to suggest movement.

The site, rediscovered in the early 1990s, is reckoned to date from between 22,000 and 10,000 BC and is still being excavated and recorded. It is of such archaeological importance that the dam project, which led to its discovery, has not been progressed.

By this time, we're pretty tired, hot, and getting apprehensive about the climb back up the steep hill. Marina leads us round a more gently curving incline, and we magically appear at the clearing where the jeep is parked, after only about five-minute walk. Sometimes it's good to completely lose track of exactly where you are!

Our hosts also arrange a private tour with a local winemaker - *Quinta Daniel* - and helpfully drive us there. The tour consists of a brief trot around the impressively modern buildings, with their stainless steel vessels and shiny interiors, followed by around forty-five minutes of solid drinking. No spitting out here.

We sample a range of 5 different wines produced by the *quinta*, a large glass at a time, and are already pleasantly relaxed by the time we get to *Quinta Daniel's* premier offering.

The *quinta's* guide saves their most expensive red (15 Euros per bottle!) for last. It is excellent, though our appreciation is probably enhanced by imbibing all those glasses of their other varieties first! He tells us that he has personally seen this wine on the wine list of a swanky London restaurant for £200 a bottle. We buy one bottle to drink back at the house, and we promise to order more once we're back home in Scotland.

Between excursions, we hang out by the pleasant, bracingly cold swimming pool beside our rustic house in Bairro do Casal, with fabulous views out over the vine-clad valley. Normally, our only companions are a group of very clean-looking pigeons, who alight on the poolside to have a drink of water. Maybe they visited a local *quinta* earlier in the day. The contrast to the hustle and bustle of Porto could not be greater.

This idyll is only slightly disrupted on our final day by a loud and boorish Portuguese family who monopolise the pool and generally disturb the tranquillity. There always has to be one fly in the ointment, I guess.

I retaliate by trying to watch a Hibs match live on my laptop, but the wi-fi isn't up to it. After a few minutes of watching pictures so hazy I can barely tell the teams apart, I give up and return to my book.

We preferred it when the pool was only shared with the clever little robot cleaner which regularly traverses the water, gobbling up anything which shouldn't be there. Maybe we should have let it loose on the pool when they were all in it. Kind of Pool Pacman.

Towards the end of our stay, Fiona remarks "This is only our second stop, but it will take some topping!" She is, as always, proven to be not far wrong.

A return to Porto is required, to move on with our travel itinerary, so we have the pleasure of a repeat journey along the banks of the Douro, in the opposite direction. Back at Sao Bento station, we switch trains for the trip down to Coimbra, home to one of Portugal's most ancient and most prestigious universities.

Helpful Hints: Douro Valley

Travel up the Douro Valley from Porto, as far as possible, by train or river boat. The scenery is spectacularly beautiful. Stay for at least a few nights, to allow you to absorb the wonderful warmth, peace, and tranquillity, along with copious quantities of red wine and port.

The rock carvings at Canada do Inferno are well worth the slightly awkward walk. Prepare to be hot.

Nights are dark and wi-fi/tv can be unreliable. Take some good reading material.

Insect life after dark can be intimidating, even after taking all the normal precautions.

CHAPTER 7: COIMBRA

As we stand in the long queue for entry tickets, in the welcome shade provided by a University building, we are beautifully serenaded by the strains of *"The Bonnie Banks of Loch Lomond"*. We could almost be at Hampden Park, with the refrain blasting out from the stadium's tannoy system and from the huge crowd of football fans gathered to watch Scotland's national team.

Except that we are in Coimbra, and the people making the music are students of the University here, mostly girls. They are all wearing white shirts and black cloaks that denote an undergraduate student who is now not in their first year, in this case from the University's Faculty of Music.

The group's instruments are violins and flutes, and their repertoire is rewarded by the captive audience dropping coins onto a black cloak that has been spread on the ground beside the queue.

It is the Coimbra University equivalent of our "Freshers Week" when new entrants get to meet each other, and other older students who act as mentors, and generally orientate themselves. New First Years are teeming around the campus in the glorious sunshine, sporting brightly coloured polo shirts, and grouped according to their Faculties.

The newbies spend a great deal of time walking around singing, chanting, and clapping and generally having a fab time. In the evening, drinking features highly, and the whole experience goes on day and night for days on end.

The campus is absolutely beautiful, with its large areas of ancient paving and its superb light-coloured stone buildings.

The piece de resistance is the square in front of the University Palace, which also features a bell tower, the University's ornate chapel and its fabulous ancient library.

We are free to walk around the interiors of the University's ancient buildings, under our own steam. We get to sit in one of the historic lecture theatres. The dark wood bench seats and writing tables contrast with the lovely blue and white wall tiles, as I stand on the terracotta-coloured floor tiles at the front.

Visually attractive the room may be, but we reckon that an hour or so in these seats would not exactly be posterior-friendly!

The University is a huge attraction for visitors to Coimbra. If UK universities could market themselves to tourists as well as Coimbra does, they would open up a whole new revenue stream.

Our accommodation is a vast modern flat in a nice apartment block, right next door to an excellent and very popular patisserie/bar. Now we are at the bottom of a really big hill, and we have to climb hundreds of steps to the University campus, every time we want to go anywhere. It is, however, well worth the effort.

It's evening now, and we walk through the campus, and on down the other side of the hill towards the old centre of the town. After a lovely meal, washed down with *vinho verde*, whilst perched on the side of a steep slope, we decide to adjourn to a local bar, which we spotted on the way past, and which advertises the musical genre *fado*. This aged folk tradition is captured by the Portuguese word *saudade* which embodies the feelings of loss and longing.

We sit on high stools at an outside table, as a very young waiter brings us huge glasses of deep red Douro wine. Happily, this lad has also clearly never heard of the formal measures we are used to in Scotland.

Two younger women at a nearby table joke with him about how much wine he is serving them. He looks slightly embarrassed and a little uncomprehending. We catch each other's eyes and bond with these two fellow travellers over our mutual love of truly massive glasses of wine. We strike up a conversation with our new acquaintances. One turns out to be Scottish, from Cumbernauld, and the other hails from New Jersey.

"We really need a drink tonight!" they agree wholeheartedly. "Our hire car was nearly written off on the motorway on the way to Coimbra, and we are still a bit shaky." I suggest that further fishbowl-sized glasses of red wine will probably help.

We join them, just to be sociable and supportive you understand. They are fun and vivacious company, and we swap travel plans and stories. We wonder if a *fado* performance will actually happen. Not that long after the advertised time, we are ushered indoors. We pay a very small entry fee. The bar doors are shut and the "Closed" sign is displayed.

The audience numbers around fifteen people and I am the only man present, other than the three male band members. Around half of those gathered in the room are local middle-aged ladies and the other half are visitors like ourselves.

As the lovely female singer leads the four-strong band through each song, she talks quite intimately to the assembled audience in Portuguese and English. Mostly about how awful, treacherous, and unfaithful men are.

She looks too young to have had a lot of first-hand experience of the downsides of the male of the species. However, she is wholly and enthusiastically supported by the older local ladies, and increasingly by the visiting ones too. The chaps in the band look unperturbed, but I decide to keep a low profile in the interests of personal safety.

Being reserved Scottish folk, if you had told us that we would end our evening singing the choruses to *fado* songs in Portuguese, in the intimate atmosphere of a tiny local bar, I would not have believed you. But we do and it is fun.

On the morning on which we leave Coimbra, we sit outside the local bar/patisserie which adjoins our apartment building, waiting for a taxi to take us to the station. The debris of the night before surrounds us. Students of a range of nationalities, who have obviously been up drinking all night, are slumped at tables, staring blearily at their coffees and croissants. We hope they recover in time for their first classes. They are young, so I'm sure they will.

Other than the fast inter-city trains from Lisbon to Madrid, it isn't easy to pass from Portugal into Spain by rail. Whether the train connection difficulties are actually due to different gauge tracks in the two countries, difficult relations between neighbours, or both, we are not quite clear.

So we have to hop on a bus from our next stop, the town of Guarda close to the Spanish border, to take us on into Spain and to the ancient city of Salamanca. A stopover in Guarda is therefore necessary before we say *adeus* to Portugal and *hola* to Spain.

Helpful Hints: Coimbra

Perhaps staying at the bottom of the huge set of steps leading up to the University campus area was not the best idea. Selecting accommodation in the upper part of the old town close to the University might be wiser.

It's a university city and Coimbra University is large, historic, fascinating, and beautiful. See: **www.uc.pt**

Take in a fado performance. We loved the small local bar version. A Theatre of Fado which can house a larger audience is also available. Tickets can be booked in advance at: **fadoaocentro.com**

Avoid Freshers Week unless you don't mind noise and singing, practically all day and all night.

CHAPTER 8: GUARDA

The enormous undulating snake arches its pink forked tongue out, just above the head of the dark-haired young woman in the bright red blouse and black jeans. She seems oblivious to its presence as she descends the stairway, with her left hand on the rail, although she has only to glance to her right to see the reptile's massive scales. She looks very vulnerable, with her sleeveless top and her small black backpack.

To the right of the stairway, the scene is observed by a very young girl who is dressed in some sort of traditional light blue blouse. She has what appears to be brown aviator goggles resting on top of her straight blonde hair. The girl wields a weapon that looks like some sort of vicious scythe, as she stares balefully at the remarkable tableau laid out before her.

The little blonde girl's gaze seems to be intended to convey to the reptilian predator that, should it attempt to strike the woman, this will be met with dire consequences.

Is this a nightmare scenario resulting from too much cheese to help soak up the lovely red San Esteve wine at a late-ish dinner in our hotel? Nope, just a striking example of the urban art that features so often in Portuguese cities. Guarda appears to go in for these installations in quite a big way.

The young woman in red and black is real, as is the staircase she is descending. The rest of the scene is formed by a huge mural that adorns the concrete sides of the long, steep external staircase, and the concrete walls on either side of it. One could easily conjecture the Freudian significance of the huge image.

It is fascinating and disturbing in equal measure and is very skilfully executed.

More by luck than judgement, I manage to click my camera's shutter at the exact moment in which the real woman in red is poised immediately below the fork of the snake's huge tongue, and so it appears that the predator is about to strike. And so I've managed to capture one of the most striking images from our entire trip, while we are just out for a bit of a stroll around a city about which we know very little.

Guarda's claim to fame is that it is the highest city in Portugal (1,056m/3,465ft) and it is one of the most important cities in the Portuguese region of Beira Alta.

The large, quite empty main square, and the back streets, have a certain charm, but what stands out most is its penchant for urban art - other huge, very well-executed murals adorn a number of walls. By way of contrast, and as a remnant from the past, the square has a well-preserved arched stone arcade dating from Roman times on the north side, which now shades souvenir shops and cafes.

We walk across and up the main square in the warm sunshine. The square tilts upwards from northeast to southwest, where the heart of Guarda, the *Se* (cathedral) looms.

This imposing building was a medieval temple built in the Gothic and Manueline styles. The architect Rosendo Carvalheira restored the building between 1899 and 1921. The exterior looks quite like a huge and forbidding castle and its fiercest gargoyles face its Spanish neighbours across the border.

The most memorable feature of the cathedral's interior is its soaring rope-like columns whose strands intertwine as if they were a girl's platted hair. For some reason, these remind us of the famous Apprentice Pillar in Rosslyn Kirk near Edinburgh. Can't be getting homesick already, surely.

The next morning, as we leave Guarda, we have to rather quaintly obtain our bus tickets from a shop around 100 metres from the bus station. The bus trip is fine, though the seats seem to have been designed for people who are much smaller than me, and the wearing of seatbelts is mandatory. I feel a bit like I'm making the journey in a straitjacket.

However, in due course we cross the border seamlessly and make our first stop on Spanish soil at a vast and atmosphere-free roadside Spanish bar/restaurant, to stretch our legs and attend to the call of nature.

Helpful Hints: Guarda

Even locations like Guarda that we regard as stopovers en route to somewhere more interesting can have their own surprising highlights. It's worth even a short stroll around to maximise these possibilities.

Guarda's cathedral is definitely a dominant presence and is worth a visit.

There are a limited number of options when it comes to rail travel between Portugal and Spain. The route into Spain by bus can be long, but it is more straightforward. Helpful information can be found at: **flixbus.co.uk**

CHAPTER 9: SALAMANCA

As the bus arrives at the first stop in Spain of our trip, the splendour and grandeur of the ancient city of Salamanca peep out teasingly from its hilltop perch. Once we are in the city proper it certainly doesn't disappoint.

We get to our quirky little boutique hotel, which has very modern and disconcerting glass-floored corridors around a central space. I can never convince my brain that it's actually safe to walk on these and reaching the lift after only a matter of a few strides is always a relief.

We sally forth in the early evening, cross the road, and climb a few steps to walk through a grand stone archway. We appear unexpectedly in the corner of Salamanca's imposing Plaza Major, having not realised how close it is to our hotel.

Our timing is accidentally impeccable. As we set foot in the square and start to marvel at its architectural beauty and its grandeur, the first set of floodlights illuminating the buildings on all four sides springs into life.

As we select a table at which to sit and have a pre-dinner drink, the evening becomes rapidly darker and the second set of lights kicks in. A few moments later, as our drinks arrive, darkness falls and the third and final tranche of lights switches on. The effect is honestly quite magical.

As we sit enjoying our drinks in this relaxed and beautiful

environment, it's noticeable that many of the people walking around in the square look very beautiful themselves - attractive in a very well-dressed and well-heeled sort of way.

Hang on though, what's that sound breaking through the agreeable background hubbub of conversation? Yelling, chanting, singing, clapping. Am I having a flashback to Coimbra's Freshers' Week festivities?

No, there are no black cloaks or red polo shirts in evidence, so the groups of excited young folk must be the University of Salamanca's equivalent. They all look like school kids which, I suppose, they were until fairly recently. Their infectious excitement at the beginning of this new chapter in their lives adds to the already vibrant atmosphere.

The University of Salamanca is even older than the University of Coimbra - it gives ample evidence of the intertwining of religion and academic learning at every turn. It was a couple of centuries old before the University actually owned any of its own teaching buildings. Previously, teaching had been done against the religious background of the Catholic church, on sanctified premises.

This ancient seat of learning now occupies many buildings spread throughout the old city. Each has its own charms and points of interest. Salamanca University is one that presents its buildings, history, and ethos superbly to the visitor. As I suggested with regard to Coimbra, many UK Universities could also learn from Salamanca's example.

The city has perhaps a slightly stuffy feel during the day, and an air of *un poco* self-importance drifts through the University and the larger Church buildings which we visit. It is, however, a very walkable old city. You can simply select which ancient edifices - whether University buildings, churches, or convents - you'd like to see the inside of, without setting out on a tour that will leave you exhausted.

A particular favourite of ours is the *Convento de las Duenas*, which has a beautiful external gallery overlooking its main central courtyard. The carved stone pillars of the gallery are adorned with a plethora of finely executed gargoyles, which range from the slightly rude to the quite scary. One or two happen to sport faces that are disconcertingly reminiscent of Michael Heseltine.

The walls of the grassy courtyard below include a couple of *mihrabs*. These *mihrabs* are attractively tiled semi-circular niches. Normally found in the wall of a mosque, these niches indicate the *qibla,* the direction of the Kaaba in Mecca and so the direction that Muslims face whilst they are praying.

This is just one of the frequent instances one can find in Spain of the co-existence of features of both the Christian and Muslim religions, side by side in the same structure. More of *mihrabs* later, when we get to El Puerto de Santa Maria!

From a small opening in the wall, the nuns of the Convento also sell delicious pastries at very reasonable prices, the proceeds going towards the upkeep of the convent buildings. So, a box of those sweet treats accompanies us back to our hotel.

We select an appealing restaurant for dinner that, unlike some in the vicinity, isn't too expensive. We sit out in a small quiet square, with only the buzz of other diners' conversations as accompaniment. The menus are made from large flat thick card, and it is only after we make a few unsuccessful attempts to return them after ordering, that we finally comprehend that they double as placemats.

We crash awake at 4 am on the final night of our stay in Salamanca, our dreams torn asunder by the unmistakable sound of the hotel's fire alarm system. The siren wail stops and starts three times, which probably indicates a technical fault.

However, I've recently retired after thirty-eight years as

an occupational safety and health professional, so I am programmed not to make that assumption! Like a good safety man, I make my way downstairs to investigate, not using the lifts of course. All the way down, my sleep-befuddled brain is pounded by the throbbingly loud alarm system.

On the way downstairs to Reception, through open windows, I hear this tumultuous noise outside. "Must be a major incident!" I conclude. "Terrorist attack? Gas explosion?" The absence of emergency services' sirens does not occur to me till later.

When I reach Reception, it turns out to be only a false fire alarm in the hotel. I seem to be the only hotel guest who has bothered to investigate in person.

The tumultuous external hubbub is just the streets of old Salamanca at 4 am on a Sunday morning. Maybe that's where the other hotel guests are. When I get back to our room Fiona is snoring delicately, entirely oblivious to my overactive imagination.

Helpful Hints: Salamanca

Salamanca is a very walkable city, so be prepared to walk! The old city is full of ornate, ancient, and very attractive buildings, so planning a practical route and itinerary is wise.

The best time for a visit to Plaza Major is at dusk. It is beautifully atmospheric.

Try to include both the Convento de las Duenas and Las Escuelas Menores cloister in your visits

Salamanca is another ancient University town, so take advantage of the easy access to many of the University of Salamanca's fascinating buildings. See: **www.usal.es**

CHAPTER 10: AVILA

Next up along the train route towards Madrid is the stop which I had insisted we shoehorn into our plans, against Fiona's better judgement. Avila is one of Spain's fortified hilltop cities. I am keen to stay in at least one of these walled cities, and Avila is the most convenient for our planned route.

Initial impressions of anywhere you visit are always very important. We stroll into the centre of town and decide to stop for some food at an outside café table close to a gate in the massive city walls.

The waiter who comes to take our order, unfortunately, has a heavy cold. As he hands us menus, he appears to empty some of the contents of his nose into the palm of one of his hands. Henceforth, we know him as Snotterman. He comes back a few minutes later, coughing and sneezing.

"Come on, we're out of here!" says Fiona, in a tone that brooks no argument. Given Snotterman's apparent lack of attention to basic hygiene, we leave his establishment, intent on ordering lunch without a serving of unidentified viruses on the side.

We end up eating outside a slightly garish-looking Turkish kebab shop, which seems to have been opened specially for us, as there are no other clients. Our stomachs survive the experience. In fact, the kebabs are rather good.

Initial impressions are also that perhaps I should have listened to Fiona. A greater contrast to Salamanca is hard to imagine - Avila is a day trip destination from Madrid, and it feels like it.

The local folk we encounter seem dour and are probably sick and tired of the constant procession of transient visitors from the big city.

Avila was declared a UNESCO World Heritage site in 1985. The site now consists of the walled city plus a number of churches.

We make a tour on foot of the city walls, which are undeniably massive and impressive. If I were being picky, I'd say that the crenelated walls have been restored so well that they look almost too perfect and too gleamingly new.

Some of the high steps are a little arduous and the walkways are often fully exposed to the heat of the sun, with the temperature around 30 degrees C. However, the views of Avila, and out across the surrounding countryside, from various vantage points, are quite spectacular.

There is a beautiful white marble statue of Santa Theresa of Avila which stands, or rather reclines, by one of the huge arched gates in the restored city walls.

Theresa of Avila lived from 1515 to 1582. She was a Catholic noblewoman who was called to her vocation of convent life, as a Carmelite nun. She was active during the Catholic Reformation, reforming Orders of both male and female Carmelites.

She had also apparently been a bit of a celebrity in her home province. She then moved on to become a controversial figure as she tried to reform the laxity which pervaded her Order, against the backdrop of the Spanish Inquisition in her home country and the Protestant Reformation spreading across Europe.

We were later to learn that Saint Theresa also apparently had an other-worldly experience involving a little angel, who was apparently wielding a worryingly pointy arrow in her direction. Some modern interpreters hold that this incident may have been one of the earliest recorded instances of an attempted alien abduction, subsequently reinvented and promulgated with all manner of religious trappings by the Catholic church.

After the heat of the walk around the walls, we're happy to

enter the cool of the cathedral, pausing briefly to listen to a lone busker playing the Avilan version of the bagpipes.

We're both a bit churched-out by now, but the interior of the cathedral is undeniably impressive, and it rambles on confusingly but interestingly. The building includes a long secret passage, helpfully signposted "SECRET PASSAGE".

In the slanting late afternoon sunshine, we walk around the town with one eye on potential dinner venues. From what we observe, many of the local restaurants seem to serve up fairly unappetising-looking fare, at somewhat inflated prices. When the dog under the table, gnawing a bone, seems to be enjoying its meal the most, maybe it's wise to move on.

"Don't fancy any of these places," is the agreed conclusion.

The saving grace is that the hotel Fiona has booked, the *Palacio de los Velada*, is excellent if a little old-fashioned. The lifts are quaint museum pieces but they work well. The building is, as its name suggests, a beautifully converted *palacio*, with a covered courtyard containing café/restaurants. The courtyard features the original carved columns lending the space an authentic Andalucian ambience.

Bearing in mind our survey of the nearby restaurants, we decide to eat in a small new café attached to the front of our hotel. Always afraid of underordering, we eye up the selection of *tapas* and *raciones* which are chalked up on the board beside our table. We also select a nice half bottle of red wine for Fiona to accompany the food, having asked for *una cerveza y una copa de vino rojo* to start with.

At this point, the waiter takes us under his wing.

"May I suggest that madam does not order a half bottle of red wine but instead orders by the glass? We have a tradition here in Avila that when you order two drinks by the glass, each drink is accompanied by the complimentary *tapa* of your choice from the menu."

So, each time we order another beer and a glass of wine we also get two lovely (free) hot *tapas*, which are delicious, and large. Four rounds later, we actually have to decline the food offered, as we are too full to eat any more. This is my kind of place.

As an added bonus, first Real Betis v Athletic Bilbao, then an excellent game between FC Barcelona and Girona, are live on TV. What's not to like? Fiona somehow manages to hide her delight.

Apparently, whilst filming scenes from his 1965 film "Chimes at Midnight" Orson Welles declared that Avila was the place in which he would most desire to live. He allegedly called it a "strange, tragic place". Perhaps he too made the mistake of stopping by Snotterman's café for lunch.

Helpful Hints: Avila

Avila is historic and interesting, in a perfectly restored sort of way. A day or two visit is probably enough.

Probably better to try to avoid visiting on weekends, or public holidays in Madrid.

Remember the excellent tradition of a free tapa with each drink (though we're not sure how extensively it is now complied with!)

Like Santa Theresa, try not to get abducted by aliens.

CHAPTER 11: SEVILLA

The train then carries us onwards to Madrid where we are to board the sleek high-speed AVE service to Sevilla.

Every time we arrive at Atocha station, I can't stop my mind from dwelling on the horrific events of 11th March 2004. A terrorist cell carried out the coordinated bombings of packed commuter trains as they arrived at the station, killing 191 poor souls and injuring 1800, in a bid to influence the policies of the Spanish government. The station contains a memorial to the victims of the attack, which includes a virtual shrine.

The station's showpiece central plaza is a lovely space, containing a small botanical garden with tiny turtles living at one end. I never like the feeling of the building, however, and I'm always glad to get out of Atocha, heading to another destination. Stupid, I know, but I can't seem to shake off a feeling of foreboding whenever I'm there.

We have booked seats in a First Class coach on the AVE, which means we have the use of the swanky Sala Club lounge in the station before we depart. We relax and avail ourselves of the complimentary drinks and snacks on offer. Fiona tells me to stop being morbid.

The AVE train itself runs on the Madrid-Sevilla high-speed line, brought into service in 1992, travelling its 472 kilometre length at speeds of up to 300 km/hr. The walled city of Toledo can be seen towering above the line in the early stages of the journey. The line reaches its highest point at 800m whilst crossing the Sierra Morena, and descends to sea level as it approaches Santa Justa station in Sevilla.

Our First Class coach boasts leather aircraft-style seats and we enjoy a nice lunch on the train, with plentiful wine and beer included. The journey is fast and very comfortable. Our companions in First seem to be mostly male, and the majority appear to be working on laptops. It makes the luxurious passenger accommodation seem even better when we share it with other passengers who are hard at work whilst we travel at our leisure.

This none-too-admirable trait reminds me of an old mate, who used to live in the northeast of England. At that time he worked for a construction company.

When he had a day off work, and the weather was sunny, he used to pick a pub with seats outside, which was close to either roadworks or a building site. He could then fully enjoy his pint whilst watching other poor workers slaving away.

Sevilla is a city which we have both visited separately on previous occasions, but this is our first time here together. Some things haven't changed. It is still extremely hot. Others have - the city centre is noticeably busier, with throngs of Japanese tourists milling around all the sights and filling the restaurants in the evenings.

La Bodega de la Alfalfa is an old and traditional tapas bar and restaurant. It, like everywhere else, is thronged, mainly with visitors. However, once we have got ourselves perched on a couple of high stools at a minuscule table in the corner, it is a lively and convivial eating and drinking spot and the tapas are excellent.

We shout our order to a staff member at the bar, who appears not to write anything down. Ten or so minutes later, the 5 or 6 dishes you have ordered unerringly and somewhat miraculously wing their way to our table. The only problem is fitting everything onto the small surface available. We manage.

One thing that neither of us has seen before is *el Parasol*, the futuristic series of aerial walkways which affords great views in all directions across the city of Sevilla. We stand at a particularly good vantage point, enjoying the panorama. We are suddenly aware of a dentist's drill just above our heads. At least that's what it sounds like.

Sevilla now seems to be a favoured destination for young Japanese couples to honeymoon in, spending a lot of their time taking hundreds of photos of each other. The particular couple posing together slightly further down the aerial walkway has gone one step further.

Their friends are not only taking stills and videos, but one of them is also flying a drone, which is currently hovering a few feet above our heads. It is no doubt also recording the full extent of their joy and happiness for their Instagram stories.

The drone really does sound like having your dentist hovering just above your head, so these devices appear to be yet another means of destroying any peace and quiet which might otherwise prevail. The young couple looks very happy, however, so it's hard to be too curmudgeonly. And the 360-degree views are indeed spectacular.

Another morning and it's 35 degrees C in the sunshine. We decide to visit the beautiful Real Alcazar palace, ten minutes walk away from our accommodation in the Santa Cruz district. An hour queueing to gain entrance, half of the time in the blazing sun, does little for the general mood. We take it in turns to stand in the shade whilst the other braves the full force of the sun's rays.

However, the Alcazar is well worth the wait. It's right up there with the Alhambra in Granada, and the Bahia Palace in Marrakesh, in terms of spectacular architecture, and Sevilla's Alcazar also has extensive and beautiful gardens.

A cooling pool is backed by faded but colourful murals. Several stairs on pathways are blocked by female Spanish teenagers, who are draped across them taking endless selfies. They seem to resent their photo studio space being invaded, but you can't have everything.

On my previous visit to the city, in 2000, a mate and I had attended the fiery local derby between Real Betis Balompie and

Sevilla FC, in the (then) Manuel de la Opera Stadium, in Sevilla's Triana district.

The match had been a lively 2-2 draw, with proceedings regularly punctuated by the 40,000 Betis fans randomly throwing very large exploding fireworks (bangers, to us) into other sections of their own support. Everyone then stood up to see how much damage the airborne explosive device had inflicted.

Betis' fanatical green and white-clad supporters had kept up an almost constant chant of *"Segundo"*, to the tune of *"Volari"*, celebrating the likelihood that their arch-rivals Sevilla would be relegated to the Spanish Second Division at the end of the season. As things turned out, come the end of the season both teams were demoted, confirming that karma really is a bitch.

Michael and I later tried to find a famous flamenco club, called *La Carboneria* which occupies an old coal warehouse situated between the *Centro* and *La Buhaira* districts. Because of a mistake in the guidebook we were consulting, we had been unable to locate it, and so we headed for the quirky and lively flamenco bar *El Tamboril,* sadly now defunct.

Thanks to Fiona's unerring sense of direction (and the fact that she had been to *La Carboneria* before) we have no such problems on this occasion, and so we take in the first of two very contrasting flamenco shows.

We are immediately hit by the heat and humidity as we enter the large, but rough and ready, club. There is no air conditioning and the metalwork supporting the establishment's roof seems to be sweating. We certainly are.

However, drinks are very reasonable and, as we have arrived with some time to spare, we can position ourselves on a bench seat at a simple rough wooden table, with a couple of beers, in front of the tiny stage. A booth to our left allows purchasing of flamenco memorabilia, posters, and compact disks.

The performers are quite good, and one can only guess at their body temperatures as they play and dance up a storm. Through the years, I've learned to differentiate at least a bit between tourist, decent, good, and great flamenco. Fiona is a seasoned enthusiast, having herself danced the dance at an amateur level back home. Joaquin Cortes is a particular favourite of hers, though I'm not sure he has ever graced the stage at *La Carboneria*.

Tonight's ensemble of musicians and dancers do seem a little precious, however, as they completely ban photographs throughout their performance, and shush people intensely should they make any sort of noise.

However, the venue and the experience undeniably have an earthy charm, and *La Carboneria* is obviously a long-standing fixture in Sevilla's flamenco firmament.

Another night, we queue in the very warm evening air to get into the *Casa de la Memoria*, a mere five-minute walk from our apartment, as it turns out. The show here is of a much higher standard - great dancers, a brilliant guitarist, and at least a five-minute slot to take the odd photo!

We look around the smallish (but capacity) crowd which is arranged in a shallow arc surrounding the well-lit stage, with some overflow into a balcony area. We note that the audience members are very cosmopolitan.

Probably for this reason, many audience members exhibit quite a mixed understanding of the dance form. I'm not sure whether flamenco's *contra tiempo* rhythms are big in Japan.

So, towards the end of the show, the majority of the audience tries to join in enthusiastically but tends to clap rhythmically and happily on the beat.

Instead of being snooty about it, the excellent dancers and musicians proceed to camp up a dramatically over-egged version of flamenco to match the audience's rhythm, rather than flamenco's own traditional rhythms.

This turns out to be hilarious, and only the most rigidly inflexible of flamenco aficionados could fail to have a good time.

Perhaps there's a message here for the more precious performers we saw earlier at *La Carboneria*.

As we make the short, but still balmy, walk back to our apartment, we agree that Sevilla is still a great city to visit, with really interesting sights, fantastic bars and restaurants, and a huge buzz. It is, however, still uncomfortably hot even towards the end of September.

A bit like Edinburgh, the sheer volume of tourists can become a little overwhelming and frustrating, but then we are actively contributing to that, so I guess we can't complain too much on that score.

Helpful Hints: Sevilla

Visit the city when the temperatures are a little cooler - early or late in the year. Sevilla is a true hot spot.

The AVE train service is a great experience if you have the opportunity to sample it.

Definitely take in some live flamenco - at the rough and ready end or with a more accomplished venue and performance. La Carboneria is at: **C. Céspedes, 21, A, 41004 Sevilla**

If you get the opportunity, go to a football match, in either Real Betis Balompie's Benito Villamarin or Sevilla FC's Ramon Sanchez-Pizjuan. Be prepared for a lively afternoon, on and off the pitch!

Set aside two or three hours to enjoy the Alcazar Palace and its gardens at a leisurely pace. Book tickets online in advance, if at all possible: **alcazarsevilla.org**

CHAPTER 12:
EL PUERTO DE
SANTA MARIA

"What a horrendous stink!" exclaims Fiona, covering her nose and mouth as best she can with a hand, whilst trying to wheel her wobbling suitcase with the other.

"Oh my God, it's actually worse in here," I add encouragingly, as we enter the lobby of the building in which our flat is located. "What on earth is causing that?"

Not a great first impression of the centre of El Puerto de Santa Maria, which sits down in Spain's bottom left-hand corner. El Puerto (for short) lies at one apex of Spain's "sherry triangle", the other two being formed by Jerez de la Frontera and San Lucar. El Puerto also traditionally gives the sherry bodegas access to the outside world, via the huge, historic, and important port of Cádiz.

Fiona is particularly upset, as she feels responsible for suggesting we make a longish stop here. A fellow participant in her Spanish language class back home has recommended the city, which he visits regularly. We've decided to spend a bit longer here to relax a little, after five bigger cities on the trot.

There has apparently been some problem with the town centre's drainage system, which has caused a build-up of quite eye-nippingly noxious odours. As we have discovered, they seem to have concentrated in the lobby of our apartment building, so we make a beeline for the elevator.

Late at night, we watch from the balcony as a large tanker appears in the square and squirts some kind of foamy detergent solution into the drainage system. This initially takes the edge off the smell, which then gradually dissipates over the next day or so.

Once through the apartment door, however, we marvel at the large and ultra-modern space, which has two huge shower rooms. It does have, however, one of those automatic induction hobs. As the coffee maker is an aluminium Italian-style espresso pot, this presents a problem. Each time we try to heat it up, the hob cuts out as the vessel is too small for the hob plate.

This is just one of a number of examples we encounter in Air BnB residences that look absolutely fantastic, and are beautifully situated, but have annoying impracticalities. These glitches betray the fact that the owners have never actually tried living in them for any extended period of time.

El Puerto is bigger than we had expected and, like any other Spanish city, it has hidden gems to be discovered. It is a destination to which Spanish holiday makers go, and there's a wide range of ages and types of tourists who visit.

We have arrived at a weekend, and so have hundreds of young people from Cádiz, who pour into El Puerto town centre's clubs and bars. The atmosphere, lively at all times, becomes slightly raucous on Friday and Saturday nights, without ever taking on the edge of impending violence which can so often be the case back home in the UK.

As we walk around and sit at cafe tables, beggars and buskers are frequently in evidence. The latter tend to become familiar faces as the week goes on. This includes the lady who wanders about singing constantly.

"She could be at home in Morningside Road in Edinburgh," observes Fiona. "Apart from the fact that she's soulfully wailing flamenco songs!"

Our attempt at booking a visit by email to Castillo San Marcos, a 13th Century stronghold that is now owned by Caballero, a diverse and successful drinks company, appears to have failed miserably. After much discussion, the guide finally relents and agrees to add us to the assembling group.

One of El Puerto's major hidden gems lies within this *Castillo*. The castle's main hall features a lovely Moorish arched ceiling, which has a beautiful leather embossed *mihrab* (which indicates the direction of Mecca) at one end.

When King Alfonso the Wise took over the castle in the 13th Century, as the Moors were being chucked out of Spain, as was the normal custom he built a Christian church over the footprint of the existing mosque.

By the 17th Century, the church's altar was crumbling, and it took the supporting wall down with it, revealing the 10th Century *mihrab* for the first time in 400 years. Because King Alfonso had walled it up, rather than destroying it, it was and still is almost perfectly preserved 700 years later - no wonder they called him the Wise!

In our very modern and spacious apartment, we have a lovely shower room each, equipped with (to our eyes) a state-of-the-art shower system, which seems to be able to direct a powerful and invigorating stream of water at you, from any direction and at any strength and temperature you'd like.

"Aaaaaaaaaaaaaaaaaagh!!!" I scream, and Fiona comes running into my shower room.

"What on earth's the matter? Have you hurt yourself?" she queries, with a mixture of concern and disdain, being used to my fairly regular mishaps. She is particularly familiar with my shower travails, which often involve some degree of flooding.

"I've scalded my willie really badly!" I wail. "I must have hit the wrong button!"

A fierce jet of very hot water has sprayed out unexpectedly from a nozzle which is directly aimed at my more sensitive parts. I'm so shocked that it seems to have taken me a long moment to move out of the firing line.

I'm now hopping up and down looking, I'm sure, entirely pathetic and more than a bit comical, to the unkind observer. I examine myself, half expecting to see rising smoke.

"Set the water as cold as possible, and run it directly over the, um, affected area," she suggests helpfully. Although with a slight air of wanting to get back to what she was doing before my screaming summoned her.

So, for the next twenty minutes or so I stand in the shower doing just that, and obviously feeling like a bit of an idiot. I make an assessment as I get dressed. Things look OK, though they definitely feel a bit delicate. In the absence of any other sensible course of action, we sally forth in search of dinner.

"Let's just go out, turn left at the corner of the square, and see where it takes us," suggests Fiona. A brief stroll leads us into a fairly short pedestrian street which is packed with restaurants, bars, and atmosphere. The evening is still warm, and the street is buzzing agreeably.

We happen upon an unexpected echo of our previous destination, Sevilla. "Er Beti" is an unassuming tapas bar presumably run by fans of Sevilla's green and white football team Real Betis, who hail from the working class Triana district of that city, on the west bank of the Guadalquivir river. The interior bar boasts a couple of modest silk Real Betis pennants, framed and displayed on the back wall.

"Er Beti" specialises in serving very well-kept draught beer, and it also offers really good local wines. Thoughts of scalded privates recede into the background. The bar also serves excellent tapas. As the week goes on, we happily work our way through the menu, eschewing only the *callos* (tripe) which neither of us can ever stomach.

We like the place so much that, quite uncharacteristically, we eat there five nights out of seven. On our first visit, we make the error of asking for coffee after our meal. "Sorry no, you need to go to a coffee shop." Another evening, we ask if we could order ice cream. "Sorry no, you need to go to an ice cream shop." No frills and no nonsense at "Er Beti", a bar that clearly knows its own identity, and is all the better for it!

One afternoon, we move further out from the centre of El Puerto to investigate the outlying urbanisation and marina at Puerto Sherry. The district features a vast marina, with luxury hotels and apartments on one side of the harbour. On the other side, an ambitious housing development has obviously stalled abruptly. Occupied apartments sit cheek by jowl with unfinished ones, some with black hole windows and walls bearing liberal amounts of graffiti.

The virtual absence of other visible humans in the large area which constitutes Puerto Sherry makes us feel like maybe there's been some sort of cataclysmic global event, which we've been spared because we've been in the toilet at the time. Weird place.

Helpful Hints: El Puerto de Santa Maria

Not only a very appealing location in itself, El Puerto is also an excellent base from which to visit the other apices of the Sherry Triangle, as well as the port of Cádiz. Boats regularly leave for the short trip to Cádiz, from the waterfront around 10 minutes walk from the main square.

The centre of El Puerto is transformed at weekends by the influx of young clubbers from Cádiz.

A visit to El Castillo San Marcos is a must if only to see the leather embossed mihrab - a miracle of preservation. Perhaps best to confirm your tour by a second medium.

Puerto Sherry is worth a look, especially if you like places with strange atmospheres.

Be careful in the shower.

CHAPTER 13: CÁDIZ AND JEREZ

A 20-minute ride on the regular catamaran ferry, which leaves from a quay just along the road from our apartment, takes us to Cádiz, the historic port on Spain's Atlantic south coast. The ferry chugs along at a sedate pace until the vast port looms ever closer.

The city's industrial past and present are obvious from the heavy-duty cranes, winches, and other contraptions which litter the quaysides as we approach the ferry dock.

We have been looking forward to visiting Cádiz, and we stride eagerly across the busy dockside road and head for the imposing Plaza de San Juan de Dios, with the old town hall at its apex. We stroll on into the lovely and lively Plaza de la Catedral and (not surprisingly) approach Cádiz's massive New Cathedral.

The city does have some lovely squares, the huge cathedral, as well as other imposing structures, and very long and straight streets of unusual apartments disappearing into the distance.

However, Cádiz seems to us to be a city which tolerates visitors, just about, rather than really welcoming them, and we are increasingly glad that we have come on a day trip, rather than staying here.

As we walk through a market area at the top of the Plaza de San Juan de Dios we encounter a group of street drinkers who would not be out of place in any large British city. Their current loud good humour owes a lot to their consumption of cheap-looking alcohol as they sit on benches in the sunshine, but their mood seems balanced on a knife-edge. This makes my nervous antennae begin to quiver.

No big deal really, but it's something we don't associate much with Spain's cities. Cádiz, however, is undeniably a heavy-duty sea port, with some unlovely areas outside the old centre (a bit like Edinburgh) and we reckon that you'd possibly have to be careful where you ventured on a night out.

We tramp on in the bright sunshine towards the botanical gardens, which are almost deserted, and are a nice respite from the busy city centre. We walk on towards the colonnaded promenade looking out over the bay.

Built on a narrow promontory of land surrounded by the sea, Cádiz is one of the oldest inhabited cities in Western Europe which is still standing. Out here on the promenade, with the Carranza Bridge across the bay, you can fully appreciate the city's prime strategic position.

We decide that we are quite content not to be staying for longer in Cádiz right now, but we'd definitely like to explore this ancient European city further in the future.

We make another day trip from El Puerto de Santa Maria, this time via a ten-minute ride in a nice clean and modern commuter train, to Jerez de la Frontera, another apex of the triangle of Spain's sherry-making region.

Leaving Jerez's spectacular tiled red stone railway station, our first impression is that the town looks likely to be a nice place to explore.

We wander around its small but lovely Alcazar Palace, as the sun beats down from a clear sky. Today the halls of the Alcazar contain an exhibition of Feria (fiesta - festival) posters through the years. These are a familiar feature of many Andalucian cities. We spend some time alone in the exhibition space, enjoying the feel of time passing but traditions being preserved, in one of our favourite regions of Spain.

We move on to visit the Lustau sherry bodega for a tour and a highly educational tasting of their sherries and vermouths.

Maturation of the range of types of sherry and vermouth which Lustau produces is quite a fascinatingly complex process. At the end of the tour, we are part of a group of eight people who gather around an old wooden table in the lovely tasting room. The rays of the late afternoon sun slant through the stained glass windows of the room, illuminating the array of glasses and bottles on the tasting table.

"I think that woman is choking!" says Fiona in a stage whisper.

An older lady unfortunately appears to have swallowed some sherry which has gone down the wrong way. As she coughs and splutters, her embarrassed husband solicitously grabs a metal vessel from the table. He tries to give her a drink of water to calm things down.

I hurriedly intercept him and substitute a plastic jug of water from a nearby shelf for the well-used spittoon which he has accidentally handed to her. Not sure that would have helped matters. The poor man looks stricken with embarrassment and a very awkward hush descends on the previously animated table.

Just before leaving, we lean on the small bar in this historic Lustau room to peruse the menu of bottles that we might purchase. We asked about sending some back to Scotland. The Lustau lady's succinct reply is "Better to just buy it at Waitrose."

Helpful Hints: Cádiz and Jerez de la Frontera

The short boat trip from El Puerto to Cádiz is lovely and very reasonable.

As a city, architecturally Cádiz is a mixture of heavy industrial and visually attractive.

The visitor may not experience the same courtly courtesy in Cádiz as in (say) Madrid. Select restaurants carefully to avoid tourist traps.

Jerez de la Frontera looks to be a better bet for a longer stay. Visiting a sherry bodega may be a fairly standard tourist activity, but it's well worth doing.

CHAPTER 14: PALMA DE MALLORCA

The first time I visited Bar Abaco in Palma's old town, back in 2001, I remember it as initially quite a daunting experience. My mate Michael and I watched as the small group in front of us peaked in through the entrance, then left abruptly.

"C'mon then. We're not going to feel intimidated going into a flash bar, are we?" murmured Michael. So we decided we would breeze through the quite nondescript wooden door into the as yet unseen interior as if we owned the place.

We then proceeded to have what were almost certainly the two most expensive drinks we'd ever ordered up to the date of our visit, while we took in the exceedingly decadent ambience. A large pile of fresh fruit cascaded from the foot of a column in front of the large fireplace, spilling out into the main bar area, and flowers were all around.

A group of expensively, if flashily, dressed men and women propped up the bar, talking loudly. A powder blue suit sticks in the memory. Mullets may well have featured. We reckoned they looked like German porn stars. Mercifully with their clothes on.

In the time we sat nursing our cocktails, several prospective customers popped their heads around the door, then hightailed it away. Whether they were scared off by the general appearance and atmosphere of the place, the formally dressed waiters in their white uniforms with gold lapels, the likely exorbitant prices, or perhaps a mixture of all three, was unclear.

Bar Abaco is an old mansion house with a lovely garden area, incorporating small fountains and statues. The story goes that the house was owned by two gay men, one of whom was apparently an interior designer. When he died, his partner made the property into a shrine to their love with cages of love birds, fresh flowers everywhere, and a theme of fruit-filled abundance running through pictures and artefacts. This is how it is preserved as a bar today, and visitors can also go to the upper floor to experience the beautiful décor in its fascinating rooms.

This is our first time here together though Fiona has also been to Abaco previously, with some friends. The whole place is now rammed with tourists like ourselves and finding a table in the garden courtyard to enjoy this balmy evening is quite a task. However, we strike lucky and settle down to a Euros 18 cocktail each.

"Just remind yourself that you are paying for the whole experience, not just the drinks!" suggests Fiona helpfully.

Our experience of Palma together is also made quite different by the fact that our apartment is a flat in an old *palacio* in the heart of Palma's old town. Our mediaeval street is just wide enough to accommodate a horse-drawn carriage or a small car, with inches to spare. We had both previously stayed down by the port area, which is like a different, much swisher, world.

We check in via a clever wall-mounted machine just inside the entrance gate, without the need for any human contact. We obtain our key, and then have to leave our passports and forms in an open container in the courtyard. So much for security.

In the evening, we find a pretty and reasonably priced Italian restaurant in an ancient square that is now crammed with bars and restaurant tables. The area is lively and buzzing.

At the small dry fountain at the top of the sloping square, we are regaled by the boisterous yells of a group of street drinkers, and the occasional sound of breaking glass. This doesn't serve to make one feel all that relaxed - echoes of the centre of Cádiz. Happily, however, again no major incident ensues.

Albeit based on a brief exposure Palma, in common with several other Spanish cities, seems to have a more gentle and benevolent attitude to the poor, the addicted, and perhaps the mentally unwell, than we are used to at home.

In the morning, we decide to take a boat trip around the bay, complete with snacks and sangria. We are the only passengers for this scenic water tour, which is time well spent as the vista of the beautiful city of Palma de Mallorca's vast waterfront unfolds, with many a photo opportunity.

We have to get up very early the next morning, to take a taxi to the empty ferry terminal on Palma's waterfront, to catch our Trasmediterranea ferry from Palma to Mahón, on the lovely island of Menorca. We board the ship and stand out on deck as dawn creeps up, with its blood-red horizon almost snuffed out by a lowering anvil-shaped black cloud, which almost fills our field of vision.

We've booked a fairly cheap cabin for our 5-6 hour crossing, and we utilise it to catch up on our beauty sleep. Various working men, possibly lorry drivers, snatch some sleep on the couches in the main lounge. A number of them roll out prayer mats and begin their early morning prayers, facing towards Mecca, as we approach the "white and blue" island in Spain's Balearic group.

Helpful Hints: Palma

Staying down by the waterfront, and up in the mediaeval old town, each has its own advantages and disadvantages. Having done both, the old town wins out by a short head.

Bar Abaco is very busy, but still well worth a visit. A table in the courtyard is lovely on a balmy evening though you may have to wait for one. Take a look upstairs at the interior of the old house too.

We're very fond of boat trips. Tootling round the bay with a glass or two of sangria makes for a pleasant afternoon.

Taking the ferry between the Balearic Islands is a nice experience, avoids the hassle of airports, and allows you to polish your green credentials a little! We booked a cabin for the day, to give ourselves somewhere which is comfortable and secure for the trip.

CHAPTER 15: SOL DEL ESTE, MENORCA

As Trasmediterranea's white and red "*Forza*" ferry turns away from the squally early morning wind and rain, and heads in through the mouth of Mahón harbour, the first urbanisation we see is the small white village of Sol del Este. It is Spain's most easterly village, and so the first to see the sunrise each day. Not much sun in evidence today, however.

After a few moments, as we pass the ruined Castillo de San Felipe on our left, we approach the headland which marks the location of the La Gardenia development, a horseshoe of fifty 1970s apartments that commands a fabulous view out over the mouth of the world's second-largest natural harbour (after Pearl Harbour).

On our right is the huge former military complex of La Mola, the latest fortress dating from the mid-19th Century. La Mola is now a fascinating collection of eerily deserted buildings and gun emplacements, which also contained one of Spain's most notorious military prisons until 1970.

Further towards Mahón from the harbour mouth are Lazaretto Island and Isla del Rey, a former plague island and an old military hospital respectively, both of which are fascinating places to visit for a day trip.

As we draw level with the small cliffs outside La Gardenia's boundary wall, two small figures are visible. They are waving frantically and apparently yelling, though the noise of the ferry's engines entirely drowns them out.

Ten minutes later, we descend from the ferry, after a nifty 360-degree manoeuvre which takes us almost to within touching distance of a cruise ship moored up at the main ferry terminal for the city of Mahón. The gangplank leads us down to the secondary disembarkation point for large vessels, on the Cala Rata side of the harbour.

There waiting for us are the two figures from the La Gardenia cliffs.

Fiona's brother Brian and his wife Jo have hared into Mahón, sped along the Mol de Llevant, rounded the end of the harbour, and have arrived just in time to meet us off the boat. We'd always wanted to arrive in Menorca by sea, rather than by air, which has been the norm for all of our previous visits so that small ambition has been achieved.

Having visited this wonderful island on seven consecutive summer holidays when our children were growing up, in 2006 our family clubbed together to buy a small apartment in La Gardenia, to allow us to visit the island we all love more frequently.

We never tire of this home from home, although as we arrive on this occasion, the island's familiarity almost makes us feel as if we are one step closer to our actual home, after four weeks of travelling.

"You two look as brown as berries!" observes Jo, which is probably no real surprise as we've been idling about in some pretty hot places during our trip.

"Tell us all about the journey so far!" exclaims Brian enthusiastically. I'm sure I catch a hint of apprehension flitting across his face, just in case we do tell them *all* about our modest adventures in Portugal and mainland Spain over the last few weeks.

Trips to Menorca now involve finding one or two new things to do, new places to see, and new restaurants to try, combined with re-visiting lots of old haunts and taking great pleasure in doing so.

We're sitting, of an early evening, in the small collection of tables outside the *Chez Spir* bar, which is right on the side of the lovely harbour at Calas Fonts, fifteen minutes walk from our apartment in La Gardenia. Calas Fonts is a small, authentic Mediterranean harbour which we feel has just the right balance of its original atmosphere related to seafaring activity and several nice bars and restaurants from which to enjoy the view.

At the table next to us are four "geezer" type guys (two wearing trilby hats), who are not quite the norm for Menorca visitors. They have obviously had a refreshment or two, and are quite loud and a bit sweary, but they seem to be basically harmless guys having a good time.

"Have a lovely evening folks!" the quieter chap, who seems to be the group's host, and who has been sitting beside me, smiles as they get up to move on to pastures new.

Some time later, I go into the bar to pay our (naturally modest!) drinks bill. The bar owner tells me that the gentleman who was sitting next to me has taken care of it. After a moment of non-comprehension, we settle for appreciating his random act of kindness.

Naturally, we go back to *Chez Spir* every day for a week, but the group of lads doesn't re-appear, so sadly we have to pay for our own drinks.

There's a local winery a few minutes away from us by taxi, *Bodegas de Binifadet* where we have eaten and sampled the excellent wines they produce many times. We decide to do a vineyard tour for the first time, then have lunch and a lazy afternoon sampling their produce further.

Half the tour is actually out amongst the vines, and the passion which goes into the complex processes of wine making in boutique bodegas like *Binifadet* comes through very clearly. The differences between the types of vines cultivated in the different sections of the relatively small area covered by *Binifadet* are backed up by the palpable changes in temperature and humidity which we can surprisingly feel, as we go into a small valley or up a bit of a gradient.

We are in a group of four with an English couple of a similar age. As we walk along, I ask our young guide about Catalan politics, which are much in the news right now, and their effect on Menorca. Menorquin, the language of the island, is closely related to Catalan, although Castillian Spanish is also spoken and understood - even our broken version.

Our companions from the UK look slightly embarrassed at me raising such a potentially delicate subject with this articulate and passionate (certainly as regards wine-making) young man.

"Make no mistake, Menorca is Spain. During the Catalan Independence referendum, you see twenty Spanish flags on people's balconies for every Catalan one. The language is different from Madrid but the sentiments are the same."

I mention that I've seen a couple of Catalan flags at the *Pavello de Menorca* where the island's professional basketball club plays its home games, currently in Spain's third division, the LEB Plata.

"Yes - but only quite young people will wave them. Menorca generally is very conservative and aligns itself firmly with Spain".

I don't prolong the discussion, as our companions do seem to be a little uncomfortable with the subject, but it is interesting to hear things straight from the horse's mouth, as it were. Maybe a few of my mistaken assumptions have been dispelled along the way.

Having booked the 45-minute bodega tour for 11:00 am, we then settle down for a leisurely lunch, which for us lasts until around 5:30 pm, when we make the short trip back to La Gardenia for a late afternoon siesta. We can rapidly and effortlessly adjust to this Spanish lifestyle!

No trip to Menorca is complete for us without a visit to the *Pavello de Menorca* to watch the island's only professional basketball team compete with rivals from all over Spain's mainland and islands.

We fondly remember the halcyon days of the mid to late noughties, when Menorca Basquet competed in the ACB - Spain's top league and the second-best competition in the world, after the NBA in the USA. Towards the end of the decade, the Club kind of yo-yo'd between the top and second divisions.

The reverberations from the 2008 financial crash hit the island of Menorca hard, and the amount of vital support that local businesses could provide to their professional team, by way of advertising revenue and sponsorship, dwindled away. After a long and arduous campaign in 2011/12, Menorca Basquet won promotion back up to the ACB, but could not afford the financial bond required to make the jump to Spain's top league.

Very sadly, they went out of business in 2012, after 60 years in existence, but returned to the fray in the EBA (amateur) League in 2017. From there the Club promptly gained promotion to the lowest professional level in Spain, the LEB Plata, which is where they currently ply their trade.

This phoenix-like resurgence was very welcome, both to the island and to the Club's Scottish fans (i.e. us). So today is match day for what is probably the only game we'll get to attend this season, a couple of days before we fly home.

There's a big and noisy home crowd, complete with an energetic and accomplished brass band and drummers. Menorca has a substantial 18-point lead at halftime, which is unfortunately whittled away point by point (or rather 3 points by 3 points) by Albacete's guards, who are in great shooting form. Our lead is restored to 11 midway through the final Quarter of the match.

Things are looking good for a first win of the season! We lose by 2.

Never mind, it will hopefully serve as a learning experience for the players, most of whom are new to this League. I guess it would have been too much to hope for, to end such a fantastic trip with a fairy tale win for Menorca, but they came so close...

And so, as we approach the end of our 6 week trip from Edinburgh to Mahón, our two weeks in Menorca have flown by even faster than normal. The weather has turned out better than predicted and it looks like we'll fly off from a beautifully sunny, and still pretty warm, island to return home to a 15-degree temperature drop, no sunshine, and a Scottish winter looming. And endless news of Brexit.

Helpful Hints: Menorca

Tourism development on the island has been much more tightly controlled than on big brother Mallorca. The island now presents a very well-balanced environment.

The more touristically developed end of the island is on the western side. The east also attracts visitors but has fewer package tours.

Menorca is recognised by UNESCO as a world biosphere reserve. There are lots of lovely unspoiled locations to explore.

The island features a number of fascinating megalithic archaeological sites, which are strewn across the landscape. Some have been developed for tourism whilst others sit overgrown in farmers' fields. Talati de Dalt, Trepuco, and Torre d'en Gaumes are three of our favourites, but there are many more.

If you can, take in a sporting event during your visit. Basketball wins over trotting races for us, but both sports have their dedicated aficionados.

Mahón has blossomed into a cultured city, with excellent restaurants and bars. Saturday nights are buzzing but friendly and safe.

We could wax lyrical about our favourite island forever and a day. If you haven't been, go and discover Menorca for yourself!

CHAPTER 16:
BETWEEN BIG TRIPS

Back in the 1980s and beyond, there was a vogue amongst people we knew to talk about, and sometimes practice, the art of travelling on a very low budget. The notion was to attempt to live like a local, in Delhi or Siem Reap or Quito or Marrakesh.

This would involve, for example, staying in insect-infested hostels and hotels, with no air conditioning. Spending entire days just chilling to conserve funds. Attempting to never pay more than a local would pay for food and drink. Laughing off severe alimentary tract episodes as "all part of the experience."

We never adhered to this point of view. Sure, we undoubtedly roughed it on occasion, in a way which would probably horrify us nowadays. We did get into heated arguments in restaurants about being overcharged by quite small amounts of money. We fell out volubly with taxi drivers, over a few Drachmas / Lira / Euros.

But we always tried to live whilst we travelled in as comfortable a way as we possibly could, within the funds available. And occasionally beyond that, to take into account funds we were pretty sure would probably be available shortly. We were both firmly of the view that unnecessary discomfort just spoiled, rather than enhanced, our enjoyment of a trip.

I can honestly say that travelling in Egypt or India or Cambodia taught us that we were fortunate to be welcomed there. It would have been a total cheek for us to expect not to pay as much as the locals reckoned they could get out of us, given the difference in our respective general standards of living.

OK - within reason.

On a second trip to Egypt, this time to Luxor in 1989, accompanied by my mother-in-law (I know, I am practically a saint) we once bargained with the driver of a *caleche* to be taken back to our hotel in his horse-drawn carriage. We had been in Luxor for a week or two already so we weren't, as he thought, straight off a Nile Cruise boat.

The bargaining went thus:

Me: "How much to take us to the Sheraton Hotel?"
Driver: "60 Egyptian Pounds sir!"
Me: "I'll give you 2 EP"
Driver: "OK - 4."

The going rate for the journey, from memory, was 3 Egyptian Pounds. When it comes to haggling, we do have standards, you know.

All of the above is intended to illustrate that the young people we were in 1980 were transformed from regarding ourselves as travellers to regarding ourselves as holiday makers. The latter label was applicable for a long period of time in our lives.

That didn't put us out in any way. We always tried to avoid, as we saw it, the pitfalls of inverted travel snobbery. By that I mean the notion that really roughing it and suffering significant discomforts along the way somehow legitimised one's desire to visit foreign lands and ensured a more authentic and thus more rewarding travel experience.

We've always felt that "travellers" were pretty much just tourists who had more time and less money. However, I know that some folk, including some of our close friends, might take issue with that, so I'll not labour the point further!

As you might expect, a number of significant things changed between 1980 and 2018, which ease the life of the traveller. The advent of credit cards for the majority of the population means that carrying unwisely large amounts of cash and traveller's cheques is now no longer necessary. Back-up and emergency funds are now available, which is very comforting, and cash can be obtained from ATMs in countries that have a closed currency.

During our 1980 trip, Fiona made a single phone call home, the two of us huddled together in an aged wooden booth in an Athens post office. This was so that her mum could let her know her degree result, as Fiona's studies at Glasgow University had concluded not long before we left on our trip.

Happily, the result was positive, which resulted in Fiona bursting into tears and temporarily ceasing to have the power of speech. I stood beside her, very pleased about her good news, but making fairly frantic, silent "let's move things along" gestures before her call used up our entire budget for the day.

The advent of mobile phones also means that we never feel too much out of touch with family and friends, and we can phone and message each other when necessary whilst we are away. The ability to make urgent or emergency contact is also very welcome. None of this was possible back in 1980.

The whole point of this book is to share our own journey (no pun intended) from - as we saw it - reasonably intrepid travellers to begin with, to avid holiday makers and, in later life, back to slightly more experienced travellers again.

Not exactly intrepid now perhaps, but at least overcoming our apprehensions to set out once again in our sixties, to explore areas which we are really keen and excited to visit, and to take more time to do so.

CHAPTER 17: EDINBURGH TO MAHÓN

September - October 2019

As older and perhaps wiser people, we enjoyed our journey through Portugal and Spain by train in 2018 so much that we decided to make a similar length of trip the next year, in the autumn of 2019.

Retirement Trip Number One had gone better than we could ever have hoped! Neither of us murdered the other, and we had a fabulous time. Rather than satiating the desire for an expanded period of travel, the trip served to make us more than eager to repeat the experience.

Our thoughts, therefore, turn to where to go next and how to do it, with greater recourse to sea-going vessels, rather than trains, as the primary mode of transport, but inevitably with some planes, trains, and buses thrown in along the way.

After much discussion (naturally) Retirement Trip Number Two begins to take shape in our minds, and indeed to grow arms, legs, and possibly further appendages. The plan is to fly via London to Catania in Sicily, from where we'll catch a ferry to the Aeolian Islands, off the tip of Italy's boot.

We'll stay a week on Lipari, then five days on Stromboli, before returning to Sicily for ten days, spread over three main locations:

Taormina, Siracusa, and Ragusa. Back to Catania to catch a plane to Genoa, which will allow us to visit the beautiful town of Portofino for a day.

In Genoa, we'll then board a five-day cruise on the MSC Preziosa, which will take us to Malaga, Casablanca, and finish up in Lisbon, which means Portugal will be the fourth country we'll visit on this trip. Plane from Lisbon to Barcelona, then on to Mahón, as in 2018, to round off with a couple of weeks at La Gardenia in Menorca.

The initial inspiration for this trip, which starts off with us visiting the Aeolian Islands, was a report by Sankha Guha on the BBC Holiday programme, in an episode that first aired, believe it or not, in January 2000. Nineteen years later, his report was still stuck in my head, so we decided to fulfil a long-standing desire.

The scene in Sankha's report, in which he walks out onto his hotel room terrace on the island of Panarea, is the one that flicked the switch for me, all those years ago. Fiona confessed that Sankha flicked one or two of her switches too, so perhaps that's why the Aeolian Islands also stuck in her consciousness!

One significant element in growing older is generally that one feels less confident of one's indestructibility and more conscious of protecting one's health and safety, including insuring against potential mishaps.

These natural anxieties are not reduced by something going unexpectedly wrong with one's person in the build-up to a trip.

Around two weeks before our second retirement trip was due to start, I sat down in a meeting at our local community sports centre, where I am on the Board of Trustees who oversee the running of the centre.

We opened by discussing instances of anti-social behaviour amongst the local youth, and the police response to these. After a few moments, I became aware of a pain in my left groin. Shifting position didn't help, and the pain grew more and more intense.

I excused myself to go to the toilet. On my return to the room, the faces of my colleagues betrayed their concern at my pure white, sweating face. Fiona came and took me home.

A kidney stone it was, and I was admitted to Edinburgh's Western General Hospital, where I was scanned, given painkillers, and observed, until the stone had made its way down into my bladder, ending the excruciating pain of the little blighter's passage down my left ureter. I passed the stone a couple of days later, once I was back at home - one final brief moment of panic followed by blessed relief.

These events gave us both cause for concern regarding our next big trip. The Urology Consultant signed a letter telling anyone who might be concerned that it was safe for me to travel, and an appointment was promised for me to have lithotripsy treatment soon after our return home.

We checked that our travel insurance offered appropriate cover and made sure that we packed our EHIC cards for reciprocal medical treatment in Europe.

Not the best preparation for six weeks in Sicily and the Western Mediterranean, but we pressed on with our preparations. And so it came to pass that we boarded our flight to Catania in the northeast of Sicily, with a blue plastic bag containing several vials of oral morphine in my hand luggage, and an accompanying letter explaining their presence.

The "coals to Newcastle" irony of taking this unusual addition to my holiday luggage with us to Mafia country was not lost on me.

CHAPTER 18: EDINBURGH

We're sitting at home on a Friday evening, and I'm trying to get a ticket for a football match online for a friend. Two texts come through on my phone in quick succession, announcing that the flights for both legs of our trip to and from Catania are cancelled, due to the British Airways pilots' strike.

Our son Sean and his girlfriend Claire are staying with us, as they are going on holiday to Corfu at 4:00 am tomorrow, and we are driving them to Edinburgh Airport, which means we are awake at 5:00 am.

So, Fiona goes onto the BA website to try re-book our flights for one day earlier, the day before the BA strike is due to start. She gets in before most folk whose travel plans have also sadly been disrupted start to do the same. Many stories of people's inability to access the BA site, and other flight issues, unfold during the course of the Saturday. We've been lucky - so far, so good!

On the Monday, I go down to the Sports Centre and the aforementioned kidney stone begins its own journey southwards.

Around this point, the active volcano on the Aeolian Island of Stromboli, our third port of call on this trip, erupts spectacularly. A state of emergency is declared, in which ferry and hydrofoil access to the island is halted by the Mayor.

We email our hotel on Stromboli, assuming that our visit will not be possible. They assure us that everything will be fine.

Their response is as follows:

"The situation on the island is quiet and in total safety, the volcano's activity does nothing but increase the beauty of the landscape, in this period the island is very charming. We'll wait for you!"

So, all good there then.

Eventually, the day of our departure dawns and we drive out to Edinburgh Airport once again with our daughter Kathleen and her boyfriend Lewis, having previously said goodbye to Sean, who is now at a music festival on the Isle of Skye. We manage to find Edinburgh Airport no bother this time around, and Kathleen drops us off and departs with our car.

I take a few steps towards the terminal building from the drop-off point.

"My basketball boots feel funny," I think to myself. After a few moments, I realise that I've forgotten to put in the vital orthotic devices which help keep the geometry of my joints satisfactorily aligned. These hard rubber inserts look unimpressive but, without them, key joints progressively start to play up. Knee, back, neck. Halo.

I confess to Fiona, who favours me with one of her most withering looks. "You are actually unbelievable!" is a rough approximation of her response to my omission.

We immediately get on the phone to Kathleen. As a dutiful daughter should, she makes a mercy dash back to our house, and finds the said objects in the shoes that I was last wearing.

She hares back out to the airport, a 45-minute drive from our house on a good day, just in time for us to be fast-tracked through security (who have been alerted to a passenger waiting for the arrival of essential medical devices). We get to our allocated departure gate moments before the flight to London Gatwick boards.

So, all in all, we've had an uneventful and relaxed build-up to Retirement Trip Number Two. Now on to the home of active volcanoes and the Mafia.

CHAPTER 19: CATANIA

The *Alibus* hurtles along the bendy road from Catania Airport to the city centre, careering around steep, sharp curves, apparently inches from the metal roadside barriers. A slightly built middle-aged woman is thrown screaming from her seat on one side of the bus clean across the gangway to the other side. Luckily, she is caught by the passengers in the seats opposite, and so she avoids injury.

The white knuckle ride continues for about 10 minutes, before we arrive, miraculously all still in one piece. Once the passengers have disembarked on wobbly legs, the driver stands beside the open door, nonchalantly drawing on a cigarette.

Fiona decides to give him a piece of her mind regarding his driving skills. She gets a few angry words out, before he turns his back fully on her, and gazes out of the window.

Welcome to Catania.

We've flown here, for a single-night stay, before we head out to the Aeolian Islands and our first stop, Lipari. Because our new flight arrives a bit earlier than our original one was scheduled to, we have a few hours to explore the city.

"There's really quite an oppressive atmosphere downtown," observes Fiona. "Lots of dodgy-looking people about."

We stroll along the narrow streets which are decorated with

a canopy of coloured umbrellas suspended overhead. The humidity is oppressive and the sky is lowering.

Catania is Sicily's second-largest city, after Palermo. From its position at the base of Mount Etna, still an active volcano, it looks out over the island's east coast to the Ionian sea.

Catania has an interesting and historic centre, with a nicely excavated Roman amphitheatre, which we visit. However, it's not the sort of place where you can ever feel very relaxed.

The city's main square is very attractive, surrounded by fine baroque buildings and sporting a quaint fountain. It features a small elephant made from black volcanic lava, which for some reason has an Egyptian obelisk growing out of its back. Apparently, dwarf elephants featured in the island's prehistoric fauna from the Upper Palaeolithic era.

The apartment blocks which crowd in, a stone's throw from this historic centre, are grim and graffiti-strewn. Catania must have drawn Hellas Verona in the Italian Cup sometime recently, as the Hellas Ultras have visibly left their calling cards.

We stroll on through a large market, which appears to contain nothing you would ever want to buy. The food stalls are interesting, however, with a range of weird and wonderful (to our eye) fish and cephalopods on view.

We keep our bags close to our bodies, secured by a hand at all times. This does not prevent a local café owner from robbing us of an exorbitant sum for two small coffees and two bottles of water. When we dare to comment adversely, he also rudely turns his back on us. Must be an endearing local custom.

With more than a little relief, we board the *Alibus* once more, for the trip back to the airport, where we catch a shuttle bus to our hotel. Happily, we are at the mercy of a different *Alibus* driver on this leg, and so the return journey is less eventful.

Back in our very large hotel room, we step out onto our spacious balcony, which affords a panoramic monotone view of the local cement works. Ah well, parting with Catania will be such sweet sorrow.

Helpful Hints: Catania

We view Catania as a necessary stopping-off point, en route to more attractive destinations, rather than a desirable location in its own right.

The city has some redeeming features. Whether these counter-balance its bad points is debatable.

A warm local welcome seems to be elusive. Maybe we were just unlucky.

Move on rapidly, and head for the Aeolian Islands!

CHAPTER 20:
LIPARI, VULCANO
AND SALINA

One of the main attractions of setting out to visit the Aeolian Islands is that, when you say where you are going, the listener normally responds "Where?" or "I've never heard of them," or "Why do you want to go there?"

This, allied to the fact that it takes two flights, an overnight stay in Sicily, and a hydrofoil trip to reach them from Scotland, all help to make the islands seem just that little bit farther away and ever so slightly exotic, as compared to the Spanish and Greek islands with which we, especially here in the UK, are so familiar.

As I mentioned earlier, the original inspiration for this part of our trip was a report by BBC Holiday correspondent Sankha Guha, broadcast back in the first month of the new millennium. Something about the atmosphere which came across in Sankha's report captivated me, in particular, and the intention to go there had ever since lurked in the backs of our minds

Seven main islands make up this beautiful volcanic archipelago in the Tyrrhenian Sea, off the north coast of Sicily - Lipari, Vulcano, Salina, Stromboli, Filicudi, Alicudi, and Panarea - together with a further five more minor neighbours. The archipelago is located between the famous volcanoes of Mount Etna and Mount Vesuvius.

The island group takes its name from the demigod of winds, Aeolus. The Aeolian Islands have been a UNESCO World Heritage Site since the year 2000, They are one of fifty-five such sites in Italy.

Of the seven major islands, Lipari is the largest, and indeed the Aeolian Islands are sometimes also referred to as the Lipari Islands or the Lipari Group.

So the trip starts with a hydrofoil ride from the port town of Milazzo, which is a short, and relatively sedate, bus ride from Catania. As we wait for the hydrofoil, in the shade of a café parasol, I sample for the first time what is destined to become a firm favourite snack in the future - a rice and meat *arancino*. This filling and tasty repast, sculpted in the shape of a miniature volcano, definitely hits the spot.

After about an hour's hydrofoiling, we alight on the small dock at Lipari. We explore very briefly whilst waiting for our shuttle bus.

"It's just like walking into a 1950s Italian movie!" squeals Fiona delightedly. "Look at all the Vespas, and all the balconies bursting with colourful flowers."

The hotel's shuttle bus arrives promptly and whisks us up the steep hill away from the waterfront to our hotel for the next five nights. The Hotel Borgo Eolie is a wonderful boutique hotel, beautifully designed and kept, with an idyllic kidney-shaped pool. Idyllic apart from the wide range of biting insects that appear to have taken a particular liking to me, presumably because I am so fragrant.

The hotel runs the best (free) shuttle bus service ever, and they are happy to take us wherever we want to go, at practically all times of the day and night, and pick us up again at the end of an evening. Which is great, because we don't fancy toiling up that long steep hill, after a good meal and a few glasses of a nice Sicilian red wine, its full body assisted by the plentiful nutrients the vine has drawn up from the island's rich volcanic soil.

Walking around Lipari town definitely feels like taking a step back in time. As Fiona enthusiastically observes, Vespas and Lambrettas are everywhere. Balconies, often festooned with vibrant swathes of flowers, almost touch across almost claustrophobically narrow alleyways. Tickets for boat trips are still slips of paper, and almost everyone is relaxed, friendly, and helpful.

Time doesn't seem to be of much consequence. One boat trip we take dawdles back well over an hour late, in the warm glow of the low late afternoon sun, but nobody seems to mind. We recline on the bench seats sipping *Malvasia*, a sweetish sherry-like local wine, from an unlabelled bottle stowed in the aged cool box under the wheel.

Always keen to potter around on the water, we take a couple of all-day boat excursions from Lipari, the first to the island of Vulcano, named so for fairly obvious reasons. Comfortingly its last eruption was in 1890.

Whilst the excursion boats beside us in Lipari harbour are crammed with people taking trips to other islands, for some reason we seem to be the sole passengers on ours, which is nice.

The scenery on Vulcano is beautiful, with several large volcanic mounds speaking to its geological past. The main attraction is the island's volcanic mud pools, which you are encouraged to sample for their alleged health benefits.

The mud is (unsurprisingly) radioactive, and the strong sulphur content apparently ruins your swimwear. We watch from the shade at the side of the mud springs, as people cake themselves and each other in the thick, milky grey substance, whilst exposing themselves to the boiling midday sun. I'm sure the mud's application is very healthy, in a radioactive and corrosive sort of way.

The second trip is to Salina, the second largest of the Aeolian island group. A very small boat this time, with a great pilot/guide and only nine passengers. Because everyone is so friendly, we get on really well and most of us have lunch together - *cunzatu*: massive toasted slices of bread piled with tomatoes, cheese, olives, capers, anchovies, etc. - at a restaurant on the beach side.

One young woman on board the boat mentions that she has recently graduated in Architecture from the University of Milan She shares with everyone her obvious pleasure at revisiting the islands on which she enjoyed family holidays as a small child.

At one point the boat draws into a small bay, which has steeply rising rocky sides, into which have been cut tiny cave-like entrances. These former dwellings are now used as boat houses. This was the location of the 1994 film "*Il Postino*" (The Postman). The movie tells the story of the exiled Cuban poet, Pablo Neruda, who comes to live on Salina. It recounts his effect on the life of the island's young postman, and the story of the latter's working-class struggles as well as his wooing of the local barmaid.

For me, Lipari itself feels very like a Greek island, perhaps a Cycladic one, thirty years ago, when we first visited that wonderful part of the world. The pace of life is agreeably slow, and mainstream package holiday companies don't seem to include the Aeolian Islands on their schedules.

They say you can never successfully revisit your first-time experiences, but Lipari unexpectedly cocoons us in feelings similar to those we experienced on islands like Mykonos, Santorini, and Paros in years gone by.

The people we meet are similar types of travellers to ourselves, who obviously enjoy the same kinds of things - a slow, relaxed way of life, friendly local people, abundant sunshine, great food, and excellent wine.

To be fair, the food and wine are significantly better on Lipari than they were on the Greek islands I'm talking about, though prices are relatively a bit higher here. Or maybe our expectations have just risen a bit more alongside the funds we have available.

Most of our fellow visitors are German, Scandinavian, or, perhaps surprisingly, Australian, with only a few Brits in evidence. Lipari is still a bit of a well-kept secret in the UK, despite Sankha Guha's efforts on BBC Holiday, all of nineteen years ago!

"It's nice to feel like island hoppers again! Even 60+ ones," murmurs Fiona, wistfully.

Helpful Hints: Lipari, Vulcano, and Salina

The Aeolian Islands are a little awkward to get to, but they are well worth the effort!

We felt we made the right decision in spending a longer time on wonderful Lipari, with day trips to the other two islands

Lipari is very different from Sicily, in a good way! It is a bit more expensive, however.

Boutique hotels like the Borgo Eolie are more intimately charming and idiosyncratic than their neighbours which may have more stars to their names.

Boat trips around and between islands allow you to enjoy the spectacular scenery. Don't always head for the bigger, busier craft - there may be smaller ones equally willing to take you.

CHAPTER 21: STROMBOLI

When approaching an island that is pretty much just a live volcano, with some houses and a few hotels scattered around its base, personal safety is understandably prominent in one's thoughts.

So it is gratifying to board the hydrofoil from Lipari to Stromboli, and immediately be invited to view the safety presentation on the video screen at the front of the vessel. For the entire hydrofoil crossing, the words *"Geen Signaal"* - no signal, in Dutch - track across the screen.

The sky is dark and lowering as we step off the gangway and onto the small jetty. We look up towards the volcano towering above us. It looks menacing and unpredictable. It's hard to tell where the clouds stop and the smoky gases rising from the volcano's crater start if indeed there is any division between the two.

Faced with this epic grandeur, a more mundane matter impinges upon my thoughts. I've put my hand in my pocket and discovered that, even though it is attached to a large wooden fob bearing our room number, I've managed to bring our room key from the Borgo Eolie with us to Stromboli.

We trail behind the other passengers from the hydrofoil as they head for the golf cart taxis which are waiting by the jetty. I telephone our hotel on Lipari and confess my sins.

A complicated arrangement for the return of the key is arranged, which involves us dropping it off to a hydrofoil crew member in the morning. This is likely to be awkward logistically, expensive in terms of taxis, and sounds unlikely to succeed.

Fiona favours me with another of her "You are actually unbelievable!" looks, which is endearingly laced with the odd expletive.

We manage to catch the last remaining golf cart and wind our way up the improbably narrow residential streets towards our hotel, expecting to be smeared against a whitewashed wall at any moment. Walls, doorways, steps, bushes, hanging plants, roadside shrines, and the odd pedestrian scrambling for cover, flash by.

Our hotel has a huge and very nice swimming pool.

Encouragingly, at one end of the pool, a sculpted figure reclines on its side, gazing into the water of the pool. It looks exactly like a black lava version of the poor people who were instantly turned to stone when Pompeii was devastated by the eruption of Vesuvius in AD 79. We hope to meet with a happier fate during our stay on Stromboli.

Our room, located in apartments separate from the main hotel building, is quirky and quite large. However, it has no storage space whatsoever, other than a few coat hangers on a rack above the fridge, and a safe. No wardrobe, no cabinets, no drawers, no shelves.

"Do you think we've booked into a nudist hotel?" I quip wittily.

"Sitting on that large expanse of cold blue tiles would be a chilling experience," observes Fiona acidly. "Not to mention a gritty one too, as it's covered in a thin layer of black ash." She demonstrates with a sooty finger.

Every surface, as we are to find out, gains its volcanic ash layer throughout the day and night, which then disappears once the cleaners have done their work, only to continually re-appear as the mountain belches at us.

On arrival, our hotel receptionist tells us that there are no restaurants in the residential district in which we are located. Once we are in our room, Fiona gets onto Google Maps and finds one a mere four minutes' walk away.

We have some of the best pasta we've ever eaten. Pity I have come out without any means of payment.

There are no cars on Stromboli, and practically no streetlights. Given the absolute certainty that I would get lost on the walk back through the pitch-black backstreets to our hotel, Fiona volunteers to go and get some money.

I settle down to enjoy my brandy, whilst I gaze out over the black waters beyond the barely visible shoreline. No one seems to be particularly phased by the considerable delay in us settling our bill.

Stromboli's obvious claim to fame is that it is home to Mount Stromboli, one of Italy's three active volcanoes. In ancient times, people believed that this mountain was where Aeolus, the demigod of the winds, lived.

Mount Stromboli erupts with some regularity. Our hotel has a live video feed from the crater, via a monitor on a desk just outside the breakfast room, just in case guests momentarily forget where they are. Eruptions are visible from many points on the island, and from the sea surrounding Stromboli, particularly thrillingly at night. Although we never heard anyone refer to it as such, the island has apparently been known as the "Lighthouse of the Mediterranean."

Gaseous emissions from Mount Stromboli are measured by a system of gas analysers, which (hopefully) detect the gasses which are given off by the rising magma, in advance of an eruption. This system allegedly improves the scientific prediction of impending volcanic activity.

On 3rd July 2019, just before 5:00 pm local time, two major explosive events, plus around twenty more minor ones, were detected by the Italian National Institute of Geophysics. A hiker on Mount Stromboli sadly died after being hit by flying rock debris at the beginning of the first eruption, and six further people suffered minor injuries during the event.

Mid-morning on 28th August 2019, an explosive eruption resulted in a flow of red-hot lava down the north side of the mountain and into the sea. The lava continued on for several hundred metres before it collapsed, sending a column of ash over 6,000 feet into the air.

We were fully aware of these events in the build-up to our departure for Sicily in September 2019 and so, unlike our lack of awareness of the political situation in Syria in 1980, we had no excuse for not being prepared (at least mentally) for Stromboli!

The volcano is indeed quite inescapable. As we sit in the shade by the pool, it towers over the landscape, regularly emitting steam or grey/black smoke. These visible emissions are usually accompanied by a not-too-distant thunder-like rumble.

This serves to act as a fairly constant reminder that natural phenomena potentially causing death and destruction are never far away. It must indeed take a special mindset on the part of the island's inhabitants to get on with the minutiae of their daily lives, literally in the shadow of the fiery mountain.

One evening, we have to retreat indoors as a quite violent thunderstorm batters the island, threatening to blow the pool furniture into the sea. Vertical stair rods of water batter off the surface of the pool, in which we had earlier swum in the hot sunshine. There is constant thunder and lightning, and high winds to keep the lashing rain company. Stromboli certainly seems to be the right place to see physics and geophysics in action.

Stromboli by night is even more spectacular than Stromboli by day. We decide to have an early dinner in a nice restaurant at the end of the town beach, which actually overhangs the sea. We have to wait half an hour for it to open and we are the only customers.

We're taking a much-anticipated night trip by boat to see the volcano. This does not disappoint! The lack of cars and streetlights on the island means that, by our 9:00 pm departure time, there is as close to zero light pollution as you can get.

Other travellers visiting Stromboli, who clearly have researched this sort of thing before arriving, wander about with miner's lamp-type things strapped to their foreheads. We just lurk about in the darkness scaring everybody.

We wait on the dark jetty until a tiny rib appears from the blackness. Our only companions are a very friendly and enthusiastic German couple, as we head out into the oily black bay, towards the nearest dimly looming headland.

Our entire field of vision is taken up by the inky black sea, a canopy of the unfathomably 3-D heavens, with stars behind stars in the sort of night sky we haven't seen for decades and the looming dark shape of the volcano. Against the spectacular sky, in one direction, a large moon appears to be suspended an inch above the horizon. On the other bow, the outline of Stromboli's volcano lurks against the starry backdrop.

Our night vision improves and, the closer we approach, the more we can see of the activity within the volcano's crater above. There is a constant fizzing orange-red fire within the crater, that looks like a giant brazier, throwing off "sparks", which are actually molten lava, around 3000 feet up from sea level, but 8000 feet from the mountain's base.

At intervals, the dark beast emits a spectacular red plume vertically, at our (very rough) guess hundreds of metres high above the rim of the crater. Sometimes this is accompanied by a more diffuse red spray of fiery lava, which can then be seen tumbling down the crater and the upper slopes of the mountain.

These visual phenomena are sometimes accompanied by an eerie silence, with only the sea lapping around the sides of the rib for aural company. On other occasions, the mountain's fiery emissions are followed by an ominous thunder rolling out across the calm sea towards the watching craft.

The four of us sit in awed silence, watching physical events which none of us has ever experienced before. Our pilot/guide says little, allowing us to appreciate these wonders of geophysics, with which he is so familiar, without interruption.

The rib's skipper is indeed a quiet chap, who seems happy to sit quietly at anchor whilst we gawp at the sound and light show that is being played out in front of us. He mentions that he recently helped evacuate the inhabitants of Ginostra, a village of 50 inhabitants in the southwest of the island, during the recent major eruption which tragically claimed the life of an Australian hiker.

He speaks in a matter-of-fact way, because clearly life beside a very active volcano requires a certain mindset, which presumably includes a dark recess in which lies the knowledge that sudden devastation is a constant possibility.

The advertised tours we looked at before we left home mentioned the opportunity to view lava flowing down the mountain and into the sea.

"Too dangerous tonight," the pilot tells us, so we cannot approach the most spectacularly active face of the volcano at present. None of the handful of other small boats proceeds beyond the headland, but at least ours is the closest to the shore.

We return to the town, enthralled by one of the most amazing experiences we have ever had. We take leave of our German friends on the quayside. They tell us that they are going to Lipari next, where they'll stay at the Hotel Borgo Eolie. We arrange to get our old room key to them tomorrow, which they very kindly promise to return to the hotel reception for us. Problem solved, by way of a happy coincidence!

The next night, we book a table for dinner at the *Osservatorio* (Observatory). This involves a short walk in the dark from our hotel's side entrance to a rendezvous point from where we catch the restaurant's shuttle bus.

After a long wait, standing in a small square along with a

few other visitors, who are just murky shapes against the whitewashed walls, a minibus arrives. Perhaps microbus would be a better description. It looks like a minibus that someone has shrunk in the wash.

We make the steep 15-minute climb up a track that seems to be narrower than the vehicle itself, as we ascend the lower slopes of the volcano. Tree branches and bushes intrude into the bus through the open windows, and you constantly feel as though the bus is going to scrape along the wall on one side or topple down the dimly discernible drop on the other.

Eventually, we arrive, to find a restaurant that has tables set out on two large, flat paved areas full of people, on which all of the seats face upwards towards the volcano's crater. At regular intervals, either vertical plumes of orange fire or sprays of lava shoot upwards, and the most spectacular moments come when the rivulets of molten lava cascade downwards from the cone-shaped peak, red against the black mountain and the obsidian night sky, in classic volcano style.

At night, these phenomena prove very hard to photograph, without decent equipment and a tripod, but totally engrossing to watch. We enthusiastically consume the wholesome pizzas and pasta on offer, accompanied by eminently quaffable red wine, whilst gazing upwards at nature in action. Happily, and quite refreshingly, we find that this unique place doesn't take the opportunity to rip visitors off due to its incredible selling point!

Most other diners appear to be German and are dressed in expensive-looking walking gear, with poles and headlamps. Some have indeed brought along equally expensive-looking SLR cameras and tripods.

I reflect that sometimes it's good not to be able to take photos of an amazing sight. I feel it makes you concentrate on the moment, rather than on recording it for posterity. Fiona is always telling me that that is a weakness of mine, and she's probably right.

With the walkers in mind, from our (hopefully!) relatively safe table, we have to marvel at the people who, in the pitch black of 10:30 pm on a Stromboli night, on treacherous paths and with only headlamps to light their way, are still winding their way up towards the crater on foot, most apparently without the benefit of a guide. This is not encouraged locally.

We can see their little lights dotting upwards, ever closer to the superheated molten rock flowing downwards towards them.

"They remind me of the folk who climb onto the sea wall, to check up close on how bad the storm is," I say distractedly. Fiona settles for a disbelieving shake of her head. Hopefully, they all survive intact, foolhardy though their behaviour looks to us.

The trip back down to the town is cramped but convivial, mainly because all of the occupants of the microbus are in various stages of inebriation. We suspect that even the driver may have had a wee bevvy.

"My record load," he proudly regales the six of us who are currently crammed into the vehicle, "is 14 Dutch people. Some of them had to lie horizontally under the roof," he grins maniacally.

Undeterred, we are so impressed by our first visit to the *Osservatorio* that we decide to repeat the experience the next night. On this occasion, the volcano's emissions are less frequent, but more powerful in terms of the vertical flumes and cascading orange-red lava which flows down from the crater.

The microbus driver suggests that "The mountain is happy tonight!" I know I seem to have gone on about the volcano a lot, but at the time of our visit to Stromboli I'm 64 years old, and I've never seen anything like it in real life.

Elsewhere in Italy, we have peered into the steamy crater of Mount Vesuvius, viewed Mount Etna from the Greek Theatre in Taormina, and crossed the caldera by boat at Thira on Santorini, before approaching on foot the gently smoking volcano opposite that spectacular Cycladean town. We even live less than a mile from the extinct volcano of Arthur's Seat in Edinburgh, which we can see from our windows.

However, the *Osservatorio* is undoubtedly our most unique and bizarre dining experience ever and, as an island, Stromboli is something else.

Out to sea, around two kilometres northeast of Stromboli, lies the other-worldly *Strombolicchio*, a sea stack of volcanic origin, which is a volcanic plug of immensely hard compacted basalt, that has resisted erosion. The tiny island with its lighthouse is the only remnant of the original volcano, from which Stromboli arose.

In the intervening 200,000 years or so, volcanic activity has moved about three kilometres southwest, to present-day Mount Stromboli. *Strombolicchio* is the only remaining visible section of a submarine rock platform that connects it to the main island. This tiny tooth-like structure is home to a variety of rare plants and animals, and so it has been declared a nature reserve, with very restricted access.

The other claim to fame that the unique Aeolian island of Stromboli has is that Ingrid Bergman starred in a 1950 movie made here. Appropriately enough, the movie is entitled "Stromboli."

To our modern eye, this black and white film is now rather dated and slightly melodramatic, though Bergman's talent, charisma, and beauty inevitably shine through. Unexpectedly, it features scenes of an actual evacuation of a town in the face of a volcanic eruption.

The film, a classic example of Italian Neorealism, was directed by Roberto Rossellini, with whom Bergman (allegedly) lived "in sin" on the island, throughout the making of "Stromboli".

Their affair caused a scandal at the time in the USA, and Bergman was denounced as "a powerful influence for evil" on the floor of the US Senate by Colorado Senator Edwin C. Johnson. Bergman's Hollywood career stalled for some years after the making of the movie.

A more welcome product of the romance between director and

star was daughter Isabella Rossellini - model, actress, author, and philanthropist. One can only assume that Bergman's and Rossellini's passion reflected the searing heat and spontaneous explosiveness of the island on which their affair began - highly volcanic Stromboli!

Helpful Hints: Stromboli

Staying on Stromboli will almost certainly be like no experience you have had previously. In the most spectacular way.

There are no streetlights on the island so (unlike us) take a headlamp with you.

Good restaurants are tucked away within the residential district of the town. They can be located online, even if you are told they don't exist.

Don't miss the night boat trip or the Osservatorio. Both are wonderful experiences that are reasonably priced.

CHAPTER 22: TAORMINA

When we were still back in Edinburgh planning our trip, we anticipated that the day of travelling between Stromboli in the Aeolian Islands and Taormina on Sicily would likely be the most difficult.

It involves taking a golf cart taxi from our hotel to the port on Stromboli, then a hydrofoil to Milazzo on Sicily (though we manage to shave two hours off that bit by getting a direct ferry), a bus from the port to Milazzo train station, and a train to Messina. We then change trains at Messina for Taormina, and finally we take a taxi from the train station to our Airbnb apartment in the old town.

No amount of planning can, however, defeat the vagaries of Sicily's railway system. Most train stations feature tracks that are overgrown with botanical life, and they have no lifts.

Passengers, therefore, have to lug suitcases down to subways and then up the other side to platforms. Elderly ladies totter up endless flights of stairs, manhandling their suitcases, while station employees look on and offer no assistance.

At Messina station, Fiona approaches a friendly station attendant, more in hope than expectation, to ask if there is a lift. "Yes!" he replies with a smile. "It's on that platform over the tracks there."

Red and white striped scaffolding barriers have been erected between the sets of tracks to stop passengers from taking their luggage the shortest route between platforms. Sometimes (I guess) this route may have had fatal consequences. As far as we can see, if you are disabled or infirm, you can forget about travelling by train in Sicily.

Added to these difficulties, trains routinely run hours late, or not at all.

The first leg of our rail trip into Messina goes OK, apart from all the station stairs. We arrive to find that our train from Messina is delayed. After a considerable wait, it is announced over the tannoy, but not on the departure boards. We hurry to the allocated platform, where we're encouraged to board a local train which will take much longer to get to Taormina, so we do.

Our original train is then announced, so we clamber off and get onto it. This train is airy, cool, and almost empty. And as far as we know, it still hasn't moved. "No power" is the final message from a harassed conductor.

The slow train has left by now, so down we descend into the subway yet again, together with a gaggle of very unhappy local folk, one of whom is a very imposing priest in full regalia. Even he seems to be unable to summon up the assistance required to get a train to run to Taormina.

We eventually arrive at Taormina's beautifully ornate railway station two hours late, with only time for a couple of beers and a sandwich before bed. Take the bus.

Taormina is a beautiful city, which has experienced Greek, Roman, and Arabic rule, presumably amongst several other occupiers. It has been a destination on the tourist route for centuries, featuring on the Victorian Grand Tour, as well as other popular itineraries. After the unification of Italy, the city began to attract moneyed visitors from Northern Europe and acquired a reputation for welcoming artistic souls.

The old town is built on an ancient site about 250 metres above the sea. From our apartment's balcony, we have an excellent view of another severely steep and somewhat isolated rock, with a Norman Castle at its peak, around 150 metres higher still. The old town is very pretty and very compact, centring on the Corso Umberto I, which is good if, like us, you have limited time to explore the city.

The views from the old town down to the sea and the port are stunning - even more so on a clear day, which we don't experience. We walk around sweating heavily in the overcast and very humid conditions.

In the other direction, Mount Etna looms imposingly large, with its crater usually obscured by clouds. It is a barely visible shadow when we are in a good position to see it, from the spectacularly situated Greek Theatre. The theatre appears to have been mostly built from brick, which suggests that it is likely actually a Roman structure, over-built on the plan of an older Greek auditorium.

At the end of a tiring day, perspiring our way around the old town and the Greek Theatre site, we scout out a nice-looking place for dinner. Our criteria are mainly that it has a good outdoor seating area, in a back street a bit off the main thoroughfare.

After a bit of a rest, we sally forth in the evening and head for our chosen restaurant. Unfortunately, the rain begins to fall, knocking on the head our plans to eat outside. So instead we are tucked into a table in a hot little corner, for a meal of what I would describe flatteringly as cheap and cheerful Italian food.

As we sip a cooling local beer, we have a chance to admire the unusual décor. What at first sight seem to be large framed prints of well-known Impressionists and later paintings, on closer inspection turn out to be re-paintings of the original works. Not so identical as to be passable off as the originals, you understand, just faithful tributes. This is a first for us - maybe it's a Sicilian custom.

Our food has just arrived, and so has the entertainment. A young man with a large ghetto blaster for accompaniment appears a few feet from our table. He has a surprisingly excellent voice, as he powers out arias from well-known operas. He also has the sweatiest shorts imaginable, which makes me feel better about the perspiration running down the back of my neck. Even the locals are finding the weather a bit close.

We stop for ice cream after our meal, at a small emporium, which has a couple of tables outside. These totter on the steep steps which form the alleyway. It also has an obscenely large plaster *cannolo* - Sicily's delicious tubular pastries, which have a sweet creamy filling - fixed on the external wall. I go in and order our very large ice creams.

As I idly gaze at the walls of the waiting area, the theme of unexpected wall coverings is continued. This establishment favours several framed vintage black and white photographs. These pictures feature naked, and clearly rather well-endowed, young men reclining on rocks beside the sea. Strange, I think, when lots of kids will be standing around in here. Well, just sort of strange anyway, in an ice cream parlour.

Our apartment is very unusual. Surely not too many Airbnbs feature an original Roman well within the apartment, behind a glass door at ground floor level. The door is openable, and small offerings, flowers, candles, etc. have been placed inside.

We hope that the Roman Gods are not too offended by the constant cursing, as we squeeze up the way-too-narrow spiral staircase between the house's three floors. There is a single room on each floor, but with a great balcony at the top level, which looks down on the ancient streets.

There are plenty of things to see and do in Taormina, which

our single full day doesn't allow us to fully explore. Maybe we'll manage that on our next visit. By then either we'll have lost weight, or we'll stay somewhere that doesn't have a tight spiral staircase to negotiate!

Helpful Hints: Taormina

The Sicilian railway system is not for the faint-hearted. Long delays, frequent cancellations, and a lack of passenger information are standard.

If you have physical disabilities or just a bad back, consider another form of transport around the island.

Taormina is very pretty, but also very busy with tourists.

Send an adult in to buy the ice creams, just in case!

CHAPTER 23: SIRACUSA

By Sicilian standards, the rail trip from Taormina's quite opulent railway station to Siracusa's more modest one is relatively straightforward. Our Airbnb host Marcello picks us up at the station and drives towards the island of Ortygia, the oldest part of the city of Siracusa, in which our apartment is located.

He asks us where else we have been in Sicily. We mention Taormina and Catania.

"Taormina - very beautiful and historic. Very busy," he responds. "Catania..." he searches for the right words, "... everyone very tense and uptight. Not so nice." We concur readily.

"But Siracusa - very relaxed and friendly. Not so many tourists. You will like." We smile and nod enthusiastically.

As we get nearer to our apartment, the streets get narrower and crumblier.

"We walk from here. Not far," says Marcello, as we alight from his little Fiat into the strong sunshine. We walk the final hundred metres along narrow streets, sweat already breaking out in the Mediterranean heat, as we trundle our suitcases awkwardly behind us.

Along the way, it surprises us as Marcello greets several local men in the street and introduces us to them. This includes the local fruit and vegetable vendor, whose tiny cave-like shop is pointed out to us. After a few moments of non-comprehension, we realise that he is establishing the fact that we are his guests and should be treated accordingly.

This, we soon discover, is because the half of the long narrow alleyway in which our apartment is situated seems to be the last bastion of the Siracusa Ultras. The gang members have recently crafted some quite well-executed graffiti in an attractive blue, marking their territory, just opposite the apartment. The Young Team members spend much of the day hanging in the street, mostly talking very fast on their phones. Sitting on the front step of our apartment is a favoured position.

Initially, the boys swagger about in a slightly intimidating manner, some wearing their blue Siracusa Ultras t-shirts. The most fearsome-looking individual is a very hard-faced young woman. She shouts constantly and is always accompanied by an even harder-looking dog.

However, the gang members seem to get used to us, and as time passes we almost get comfortable with them. Every time we pass them in the street or come back to find them sitting on our doorstep, they are unfailingly respectful and polite to us. A cheery "Buona Serra!" is offered, whenever our paths cross, which is two or three times a day.

Each evening after dark, everyone in the vicinity seems to spend their time yelling loudly at everyone else, in the street and between houses, and revving their scooters. And, it seems, standing on the fearsome dog, which omits a constant cacophony of strangled yelps. Sometimes it seems like a violent incident is on the verge of breaking out, but in the end, nothing untoward happens.

Gentrification is encroaching rapidly in Ortygia, with nice restaurants, modern bars, swish shops, boutique hotels, and, yes, Airbnbs popping up amongst the previously derelict buildings.

Our apartment is fantastic. It is new, modern, fully equipped and very comfortable indeed. The houses opposite, whose balconies almost touch ours, are in a terrible state. Some have large holes in the roof, and open gaps for windows. They look generally highly unsafe, structurally and otherwise.

Whilst the march of progress is inevitable, we feel sorry for the young people whose families have presumably always lived in Ortygia, and who are fiercely loyal to their shrinking home territory.

They spend almost all day just hanging out in the street as if they stand ready to defend their last bastion when someone comes along to build another boutique hotel, or to renovate another crumbling building for holiday lets. It seems clear that their domain will soon shrink to nothing, and who knows where these families will go then.

As I've already mentioned, Ortygia is a small island that is the historical centre of Siracusa. It's also sometimes known as *Citta Vecchia* (Old City), and we are told that its name derives from the Greek word for "quail".

The island features in Greek mythology, but rather confusingly. The identities of which God did what where are murky, not least because of the number of ancient locations which went by the name of Ortygia.

Ortygia is separated from the eastern end of Siracusa by a narrow channel, currently connected to Sicily by a couple of bridges. As it is an island close to the coast, reached by bridges, Ortygia in ancient times lent itself to the role of a natural fortress, with convenient harbours.

2,700-year-old Siracusa has a rich Greek and Roman history and the city was the birthplace of the mathematician and engineer Archimedes, famous to schoolchildren the world over for his exclamation of "Eureka!" whilst splashing about in the bath one day.

From its foundation by the ancient Greeks, Siracusa grew into a powerful city-state, rivalling Athens by the 5th Century BC. Later, the city was ruled by the Romans, and later still it became the capital of the Byzantine Empire for a short period. Modern day Siracusa is a UNESCO World Heritage Site.

A remarkably cheap and easy small bus tour stops a few yards from the end of our street, and for Euros 5 for an all-day ticket, it takes us wherever we want to go. This includes the archaeological park on "mainland" Siracusa, where the huge and fabulous Greek Theatre, and the smaller Roman Amphitheatre, are located.

The Greek Theatre is breathtakingly restored and is crying out with photographic opportunities. It is also breathtakingly sunblasted. Perhaps if the body responsible for its upkeep could post a few signs, telling visitors where not to tread, the constant cacophony of attendants blowing annoyingly shrill whistles wouldn't be necessary.

The Roman amphitheatre nearby is more compact and its shape is clearly discernible, but it is swathed in greenery. Perhaps it's next on the list for a fuller restoration.

The handy step-on/drop-off bus tour also takes us to the vast warren of the Catacombs of San Giovanni and Santa Lucia. Unlike the Paris Catacombs, these tunnels and vaults are now devoid of human bones since they were called into service as air-raid shelters during World War Two. However, you definitely wouldn't want to get lost and have to spend the night down here.

Just around the corner from our apartment, is a new and very attractive bathing platform where you can get some shade from the fierce Sicilian sun, and sunbeds and umbrellas are available for hire. A cooling swim in the clear, shallow waters under the waterfront walls is also very refreshing. It is undoubtedly a bit more upmarket than the equivalent rocky promontory used by the local folk, just a bit further along the sea wall, but you pay for the privilege at the former.

We take a (mostly) enjoyable boat trip out to caves along the shore, and back around Ortygia, which is well worth the Euros 15 each, although it almost begins with disaster (for the pilot).

He abruptly lowers the boat's wooden canopy as we approach a very low bridge in the harbour area, straight onto Fiona's head.

To say she is displeased doesn't begin to describe her reaction. The fact that he seems entirely unconcerned at this event amplifies her anger.

I have a fleeting vision of his sobbing family being informed that he has been found floating lifeless in the harbour. Fortunately, calm is restored, and we explore the ruggedly attractive coastline and caves with no further mishap.

Fiona has been keen to visit an exhibition which is heavily advertised via posters in the area close to our apartment - *Sculpture: Rodin to Giacometti.* It turns out to be held in a beautiful gallery space, part indoors and part out on a large terrace.

By the time we walk there, I'm in grumpy old bloke mode, so we decide that she'll go into the exhibition, while I go off and take photos at some Roman remains, close by one of the bridges which give access to Ortygia.

I sit and fiddle with my camera equipment for a few moments whilst she enters the exhibition, time enough for her to pop back out and call "Ally. You really should see this. It's wonderful!"

I grumblingly change my mind and am glad I did so. It turns out to be the best and most varied exhibition of sculpture that I've ever seen. The gallery is almost empty of visitors, and we can enjoy the pieces and the ambience at our leisure. The serenity of the experience is enhanced by the haunting music which accompanies it. The contrast to local life back in "our" street could hardly be sharper.

A surprise find in Ortygia, in a surprising location, is Europe's oldest Jewish ritual baths, or *mikveh.* Legend has it that the first Jews to live on Sicily were brought in in 70 AD, as Roman slaves, though there may well have been some Jewish inhabitants of the island before that date.

During the reign of King Ferdinand II of Aragon, the main architect of the Spanish Inquisition, Jews in Sicily faced execution unless they converted to Catholicism. Jews made up a quarter of Ortygia's population at that time, and the *mikveh* in Ortygia is one of the few traces you can still find of their presence.

Mikvehs were/are used for Jewish religious rituals that require purification by immersion in 'living water' - water that is naturally flowing. The freshwater spring which flows beneath Ortygia supplies that requirement. The square subterranean room has a vaulted ceiling supported by four pillars, which have been carved out of the limestone bedrock. A ventilation shaft also provides the only natural light. Oil lamps lit the space when the baths were in use.

The *mikveh* was unearthed in 1989, during work on a medieval palazzo. It now sits under the Residenza Alla Giudecca hotel in the heart of what was once the town's Jewish quarter, the 'Giudecca'. The baths date from the 6th century and were used continuously until they were abandoned in the 15th century.

Still in Ortygia, and still on the theme of water, once we are back above ground we manage to stumble upon the *Fonte Aretusa*, a lovely sunken grotto containing a freshwater fountain. Greek mythology holds that the nymph Arethusa returned to the surface of the earth here, after escaping from her undersea home in Arcadia. *Fonte Aretusa* is one of only three places in Europe, all in Sicily, where the gently waving papyrus plant grows.

Siracusa's 7th Century *Duomo* (cathedral) was built on Ortygia, over the great Temple of Athena, erected 1200 years earlier. The *Duomo* incorporates the Temple's original Doric columns in its walls, together with many later stylistic additions through the centuries.

Ortygia has a wealth of attractive streets, atmospheric alleyways, and beautiful piazzas, with the spectacular *Duomo* square, which is more of an opulent crescent, providing the architectural highlight. Sipping cocktails, outside a café facing the floodlit cathedral, transports us pleasurably to an entirely different world to that which exists a mere ten minutes' walk away, down by the waterfront.

Helpful Hints: Siracusa

The gentrification of Ortygia is proceeding apace so visit soon to experience all facets of the island and its culture.

Siracusa is rich in historical remains from a range of eras. Distances are small so visiting a good number of these sites is fairly easy. The step on/drop off tourist bus is a good way of visiting those sights which are slightly out of the centre.

Seeking out the few remaining pieces of evidence left of Siracusa's Jewish population is an interesting challenge.

Food in Ortygia, whether from a small supermarket or a bijou restaurant hidden amongst the crumbling ancient buildings of the island, is local and excellent.

On a boat trip, remember to duck below the level of the sides if you see a bridge approaching - the boat's canopy may come down abruptly!

CHAPTER 24: RAGUSA

Our final train journey of the trip climbs high through the Sicilian hills to Ragusa, the scene of many an episode of "Inspector Montalbano", the Italian detective series originally shown on BBC Four in the UK.

Il commissario Montalbano is the main character in this series of police procedural stories, based on the detective novels of Andrea Camilleri. Montalbano lives in the imaginary town of Vigata, in the fictional province of Montelusa, based on the Province of Ragusa. He has a long-distance and volatile relationship with his girlfriend Livia, who lives in Genoa.

I am a fan of the long-running, quirky, and atmospheric series, which reflects the pace of life far from Italy's big cities.

Returning to reality, with the possibility of non-homicidal fatality, we arrive at the typically overgrown railway station, to find that we have to cross the tracks, via a sort of disconcerting pedestrian crossing, complete with red and white hatching, flashing lights, and strident alarms.

We have a system for transporting our luggage, made necessary by my chronically bad back. Fiona takes her suitcase across the tracks, heaves it up onto the platform opposite, then comes back over to help me lift mine down to track level.

Unfortunately, she hasn't secured her case properly on the other platform, so I watch helplessly as it topples backwards onto the tracks, apparently in slow motion. For the first and only time, a couple of local men rush to help. She returns to her own case and I start to cross the double-width of rail tracks. Inevitably a train looms on the horizon, and the lights and alarms start.

Happily, we get up onto the platform beside the station exit in time to avoid being smeared across the small botanical garden growing between the tracks. We exit from the station, breathing a bit heavily, and walk out into what seems to be a ghost town.

Not a vehicle in sight and only a single human. He is a kindly elderly gentleman who comes up to us for a chat, obviously in Italian. We eventually manage to phone a taxi and are whisked away to our Air BnB in Ragusa *Ibla*.

The property is a beautifully refurbished local house on two floors, which has another, slightly more easily negotiated, spiral staircase. The space is full of artistic Italian flourishes, from the Ragusa-themed wallpaper to the vaulted and sculpted plaster ceiling, and the white candelabra with red candles. That's just the bedroom. The house is more designer than practical, but it is comfortable and superbly located, just a few metres from Ragusa's main square, *Piazza Duomo*.

The Montalbano effect has clearly worked wonders for the local economy, and Ragusa gives off an air of prosperity. The city is a dynamic and successful one and is home to BAPR, Italy's fourth most popular bank.

However, restaurants and cafes, even in and around the *Piazza Duomo*, prove to be good and quite reasonable. Our first visit to the piazza coincides with a wedding (echoes of Porto in 2018).

The beautiful and elegant bride and her bridesmaids pose for the wedding photographer, in front of a small fountain, the women looking the epitome of Italian chic. The males present have almost uniformly chiselled good looks and are decked out in typically sharp-suited Sicilian fashion. The tableau does have a little more of an Instagram-friendly feel, as opposed to the unashamedly romantic vibe of the Portuguese equivalent last year.

Ragusa seems to be a favoured day trip destination, so the *Ibla* district fills up with tourists during the day and empties to a more manageable population in the evening. We take a trip round *Ibla* on one of those slightly embarrassing wee tourist trains, which we would normally avoid. It turns out to be a brilliant way to see around the winding narrow streets, which would take hours on foot, in the heat.

It must be odd to live constantly on the side of a hill, and always have to negotiate steep steps or slopes to get anywhere. I suppose you don't even think about it if you've been born here, and even the elderly locals look pretty fit and spritely. For visitors like us, the constant gradients and the heat rapidly become a bit sapping.

Above Ragusa *Ibla*, on a second, higher hill, is *Ragusa Superiore*. Here the bourgeoisie set up a "new town" in a safer position after *Ibla* was virtually destroyed by an earthquake in 1693. From up there, they could look down, literally and metaphorically, on the poor folk who had to make do in *Ibla*. Now we can look down, to take photos of the quite stunning panorama of the patchwork of *Ibla's* houses, set against the hilly green backdrop of the surrounding countryside.

During the Second World War Ragusa, in common with many other Sicilian towns, was none too keen on the fascist regime of Benito Mussolini. Simple anti-Sicilian racism on the part of the fascist regime, and a draconian anti-mafia purge, contributed to this antipathy. Food scarcities in Sicily were compounded by local produce being sent to Northern Italy, and the island itself being put bottom of the list for food aid.

To add to these slights, local police officers from Sicily were replaced with those from Northern Italy. The replacements were poorly paid, so they became corrupt and indifferent to the needs of the local population.

When British and American troops landed to liberate Sicily, the small detachment of fascist troops guarding Ragusa fled without putting up any resistance. The local population is said to have welcomed the Allied soldiers with unbridled enthusiasm. Lucky soldiers!

A couple of days has been a good length of stay for a visit to the beautiful and historic town of Ragusa, before we have to get ourselves to the bus station for the trip back to Catania, to catch our flight to Genoa.

We ask the taxi driver who takes us from our apartment to the bus station to stop high up in *Ragusa Superiore* so that we can take the best photos possible of the city and its environs before we leave. He doesn't disappoint, and our ten-minute stop presents us with a breath-taking panorama. A photographer's dream.

When we get to Ragusa bus station, we find a notice in the unmanned ticket office telling us to purchase bus tickets at a local cafe, about 50 metres away. Fiona troops off to do so, leaving me huddled in the small amount of shade offered by a graffiti-strewn whitewashed wall, guarding the luggage. Turns out all tickets are to be purchased at the cafe, except for the journey we are making to Catania. Handy.

We eventually secure a ticket back at the bus station, for the only journey of our trip which we couldn't book in advance. Happily, we manage to get front row seats for the two-hour trip on an excellent road through the Sicilian countryside to Catania.

Helpful Hints: Ragusa

Before leaving home, watch a couple of episodes of the Montalbano series. It will help get you in the mood for the local ambiance, hopefully without the crime, however.

The little tourist train is a good way to navigate around the steep slopes of the old city.

The poshest-looking restaurant in the Piazza Duomo, nestling behind the fountain, is very good, very friendly, and surprisingly reasonably priced.

CHAPTER 25: GENOA AND PORTOFINO

We negotiate the small, overcrowded, chaotic, boiling hot little piece of hell on earth that is Catania airport.

Fiona and I chat over a quick meal which is of a similar standard to football food stand catering, Italian style. (I once experienced just that at Fiorentina's Artemio Franchi Stadium in Florence. A mate and I grabbed some food from a stall before going in to see La Viola play Reggiana in Serie A. If anything, Florentine football catering was surprisingly even worse than the equivalent in Scotland.)

"Well, Sicily has been really interesting and very enjoyable," says Fiona. "But I'd find it difficult to say honestly that I've fallen in love with the island. The Aeolian Islands, particularly Lipari - yes. Sicily itself, not so much."

"I know what you mean," says I. "Partly it's the obvious poverty and the crumbling infrastructure. You'd think that a relatively small area with this volume of tourists each year would be boomingly prosperous."

"It looks on the face of it like Sicily should be on par with the Balearic Islands, or some Greek islands we've visited, in terms of the general standard of living for the average man. But that clearly hasn't happened."

"You can only assume that the money coming into the island doesn't filter down very far. Or, if it does, it then gets re-routed before the general population can benefit from it," suggests Fiona.

"Indeed," I reply. We leave it at that, as we are both conscious of the inadvisability of commenting on such matters, particularly in public, after having only a brief and superficial exposure to a place.

Our flight to Genoa is delayed, and it becomes clear that we'll arrive after the time the hotel reception at the 4* hotel we are booked into closes for the night. We phone ahead to let them know.

"No problem sir, please just ask your taxi to take you a hundred metres down the same road, and check in at Reception in our sister hotel, the Gran Hotel Savoia."

We follow instructions, expecting to check in, then trundle our suitcases up the road to our original hotel. Not a bit of it!

We are courteously booked into a fabulous room in this ocean liner-themed 5* hotel and we're given details of breakfast the next morning, which proves to be excellent. We retire to our huge bed, feeling like the cats that have got the cream.

"We're only here for two nights. Surely they can't move us up the road for our second night only?" says Fiona apprehensively. Happily, they don't, and we get to enjoy a second delicious Gran Hotel Savoia breakfast.

We've chosen this location in Genoa to be handily placed for the railway station, which is directly opposite the Gran Savoia, to begin tomorrow's trip to Portofino. It's also handy for the docks, from which our MSC cruise boat *Preziosa* will depart in a couple of days.

We catch a reasonably early morning train to Santa Margherita Ligure, a beautifully situated lakeside resort town about 35 km southeast of Genoa. The area is immediately reminiscent of the

Italian Lakes, perhaps particularly *Lago Maggiore*, and it gives off an upmarket and prosperous air.

A previous conversation with a friend indicated that there are two alternatives for travelling on to Portofino, a rather more prosaic bus trip, or a ferry. We choose the boat, and we are not disappointed.

Visiting Portofino is another long-held desire - hatched during a holiday on the Amalfi coast back in 1984 - and our approach by boat reveals an almost impossibly picturesque port area.

The building facades facing onto the harbour are exquisitely painted, the cramped little marina is festooned with a range of small craft, and cruise boats ply their passage in the background. The harbour is towered over by *Castello Brown.*

This grand mansion house began life as a military defence structure in Roman times. Due to the key location of Portofino's harbour, the Castello featured in many naval battles between the 13th and 19th Centuries.

After peace finally reached Portofino, *Castello Brown* was abandoned following the Congress of Vienna in 1815. The fortress was formally disarmed in 1867, whereupon it was purchased, apparently for 7000 Lire, by Montague Yeats-Brown, at that time the British Consul in Genoa, who converted it into a comfortable villa.

The Baber family then purchased the property in 1949, restored several ruined sections, and finally sold it to the municipality of Portofino in 1961. The property is now open to the public.

The author Elizabeth von Arnin wrote and set her novel "The Enchanted April" at *Castello Brown* in 1922. An award-winning movie of the book was made in 1991, starring Miranda Richardson and Joan Plowright, which was filmed at the location.

We alight from the ferry onto the teeming harbour side and walk slowly along past some of the famous waterfront restaurants. The immediate and enduring impression is that Portofino is one of many places now that has fallen victim to its own beauty and fame.

During the day, when day trippers like ourselves arrive off the boats, the town is improbably busy. The actual well-off inhabitants of Portofino presumably keep themselves hidden away behind closed doors, in luxurious air-conditioned spaces, until the hordes leave again in the late afternoon.

We take a wander around the back streets, behind the harbour area. They are lovely, in a perfectly manicured sort of way. The streets remind us a bit of the main towns on Mykonos or Santorini - authentically preserved, but very clean, pristine, and shiny. At least the throng subsides a bit the further back we go.

We also know that Portofino will be very expensive, so we have decided not to be tempted to eat whilst we are here. We sit in a waterfront cafe to escape the fierce sun. A litre of water and two coffees set us back Euros 16.

I notice that one of the smaller rowing boats pulled up to the harbour side is named "Orkney Angler", stencilled on a fading green trimmed panel on the bow. That one's come a long way to catch a few small fish.

After about an hour of languid people-watching, I suggest to Fiona: "I've taken so many shots of buildings and boats, I'm going to take some photos of the beautiful people who frequent Portofino's waterfront. I'll be non-sexist about it though. Good looking men as well as beautiful women!"

No sooner have the words left my lips, than two female Italian models appear by the waterside, apparently to do a bridal wear shoot with a professional photographer. All the amateur tourist snappers leap at the opportunity to join in, and I am no exception.

I feel slightly guilty having said to Fiona that I'll happily snap some chic and attractive Italian men too. It's just that there are none in evidence right now.

One of the white-clad young ladies is dressed in a short, tight-fitting wedding dress, and is wearing fearsome heels, which she carries off with supreme elegance and poise. The other model sports a punkier look, wearing a voluminous and diaphanous white number, set off by a dark trilby hat and black ankle boots.

The models pose by the waterside, drape themselves over small craft whilst clutching red roses, or jump vertically on the slipway (only the one wearing boots), depending upon the instruction of their photographer.

This photogenic spectacle adds to a lovely, lazy afternoon in Portofino, which doesn't fall short of the expectations we have held for many a year. No doubt there are many very rich folks who live in the town and avoid the waterfront during the day. I'm sure those inhabitants breathe a huge sigh of relief when the hundreds of day trippers leave in the late afternoon.

I'm not sure I would covet their lifestyle. However, Portofino is a stunningly beautiful place to visit. Just arrange a mortgage in advance if you want dinner and a few drinks!

The lovely 20-minute boat trip returns us to Santa Margherita Ligure in the slanting late afternoon sunshine, and we catch the train back to Genoa. The city's grandeur is a little undermined by the piles of used toilet paper that today festoon the tracks in metro stations.

We pop out for a pizza in a roadside *trattoria* not far from our hotel, in the evening, as we are up early in the morning. On our, albeit brief, daytime and night-time exposures, Genoa certainly gives the impression of being an old established, and well-heeled city. It boasts many grand buildings and is redolent of old money, based no doubt on the port's maritime success.

We've had much less time to explore the city than would

have been ideal, but needs must. The enduring memory is of a beautifully situated, and absolutely massive, working port which would definitely be worthy of a longer visit in the future.

Helpful Hints: Genoa and Portofino

Our exposure to Genoa was brief but left us with the distinct impression that it would be an interesting and rewarding city to spend more time exploring.

Take the ferry from Santa Margherita Ligure to Portofino, and back, in preference to the bus.

Prepare either to spend a lot of money eating and drinking on Portofino's waterfront or limit yourself to a few exorbitantly priced refreshments. Console yourself with the thought that you are paying for the pleasure of the holistic experience!

CHAPTER 26: GENOA TO LISBON

MSC Preziosa

Our only previous experience of a cruise which lasted more than 24 hours was back in 2011 when Fiona, our son Sean and I decided to try a Caribbean cruise from New York, with Princess Cruises. Our daughter Kathleen was travelling in Australia at the time with her then boyfriend, so it was just the three of us on this trip.

We were a little doubtful as to how much we'd enjoy cruising, spending days onboard along with literally thousands of fellow passengers. Booking a cabin with a balcony was essential, so we could keep ourselves to ourselves when we wanted to. Sean wasn't so lucky - he had to make do with an interior berth.

Leaving South Street Seaport and watching Manhattan recede into the distance was memorable. So were a number of the stops along the way - the glorious Elbow Beach on Bermuda, swimming with rays near Grand Turk, walking in the rain forest and visiting San Juan on Puerto Rico, and tip-toeing amongst the iguanas on Saint Thomas.

Apart from forays to the outdoor basketball court, and to a variety of bars and for dinner in the evenings, we pretty much kept ourselves to ourselves. Big cabaret-style shows aren't our thing, so much of the on-board entertainment passed us by, by our own choice.

By 2019, we were having a hankering to try a cruise again, so we decided to incorporate a five-day mini-cruise from Genoa to Lisbon, calling at Malaga and Casablanca, into our trip. Often, in Mahón harbour, we'd looked admiringly at the clean-cut MSC cruise ships as they lay tied up to the dockside.

A chance conversation with a Canadian lady on board the Yellow Catamaran tour of Mahón harbour one sunny afternoon also awoke us to the possibilities offered by using a cruise as a means of transport (albeit luxury transport) from Port A to Port D, E, or F, rather than taking a conventional circular route back to a starting point.

So we decided to try the 5-day cruise on the MSC *Preziosa* as a taster for possible longer cruises in the future.

An early rise in Genoa, then a taxi ride, brings us to the cruise terminal. The process of registration and embarkation is remarkably smooth and well-oiled. Within an hour we are having an early lunch in the *Preziosa's* vast buffet restaurant.

The backdrop of Genoa's huge dockland area, and the city itself, ascending from the Ligurian Sea towards the backdrop of the Apennine Mountains, makes for a spectacular vista on this beautiful morning, as the ship fills up with people and prepares for departure. Some passengers are already in their swimwear and are leaning on the transparent glass screens beyond the swimming pool nearest to the stern, taking in the view.

As we look around our fellow travellers on deck, the signs do not look encouraging. Many are already making enthusiastic inroads into their drinks packages and smoking like small Victorian factories.

The admittedly small cross-section of the clientele visible to us suggests that there are fewer Italians than we expected but reveals quite a few other boorish and somewhat angry-looking fellow passengers. So far, not so good.

However, once we get into a rhythm of our own on the boat, things become more enjoyable. Breakfast in our very well-appointed cabin, relaxing on the balcony to watch the sea go by, and smuggling illicit daiquiris and wine into our cabin at sundown, feature regularly in our day. Fiona spots a school of dolphins alongside. Naturally, I'm in the shower at the time.

One of our less favourite things about cruise life is being stuck at the dinner table with other English-speaking folk we don't know. However, we go along to our allocated restaurant table for dinner on the first night, in good faith. We have a perfectly pleasant and convivial evening with two other couples, from Devon and Manchester.

The next night, as we approach our allocated table, it's apparent that neither of the couples is there (draw whatever unkind conclusions you like from that!) Instead, two people who look like they might have recently passed away occupy two of the six seats.

We swerve back to the restaurant's reception desk and persuade the *maitre d'* to get us a table for two, which works tonight, and on each subsequent evening too. Maybe a bit anti-social, but we can enjoy our food and drink without having to make stilted conversation, which suits us.

As we sit at our table for two, we have a good view of our originally allocated table. The elderly and rather inanimate man and woman have been joined by a much younger couple. The young woman looks tense and her partner looks very angry. The new diners take seats far enough away from their elderly table companions to effectively discourage conversation.

After a few minutes, it becomes apparent that the newcomers are engaged in something of a domestic dispute. She looks embarrassed but resigned at the same time as if this is perhaps not an uncommon occurrence.

His body language is increasingly angry and aggressive, and at one point I'm sure he is about to hit her. Thankfully that doesn't happen. They leave the table abruptly, and peace is restored. Who knows what does transpire, however, when they return to the privacy of their cabin.

A peaceful and relaxing day at sea is followed by our first port of call. Malaga is a Spanish city which we have previously passed through but have never properly visited. We approach the Spanish coastline in the hazy early morning sunshine.

We share a taxi into the centre of town with an Irish couple, who have paid an extortionate sum in advance for a city open top bus tour, only to discover that the queue to board one is so long it would take them ages just to start their tour.

"You forget just how time-consuming it can be to get into a city centre from a cruise boat terminal," sympathises Fiona. Malaga seems by general consensus to be worse than most.

We hop out of the taxi and walk through streets of very modern shops to Malaga's unusual main square, the *Placa de la Constitucion.* It's a very attractive space, less grand than in many other Spanish cities, but pedestrian only. Fiona persuades me that a visit to the Carmen Thyssen Museum nearby would be worthwhile. Its collection of Spanish art is indeed well worth seeing.

We decide that we'll take a look at the *Alcazaba*, Malaga's 11th Century Moorish fortified palace, from below but not climb up to it, in the considerable heat. Never being good at sticking to the plan, when we get there, we change our minds. We climb past the ruins of the 1st Century AD Roman theatre, and hike up the steep hill, to be rewarded with a lovely, tranquil setting and great views from the citadel.

You could feel that the *Alcazaba* is like a poor man's Alhambra, in Granada. The stucco work and other decoration here are more modest and on a much more compact scale. However, we feel it's well worth the sweaty uphill slog. It's quiet and tranquil and we can even see our cruise ship out in the bay, from this high vantage point beside a small but lovely Andalucian courtyard garden.

We always experience a bit of anxiety about (literally) missing the boat, so we descend in plenty of time to sit and watch some exotically coloured birds flitting around a small fountain, in the gardens opposite the port.

We hail a taxi which gets us back along to the *Preziosa* in good time before we are due to depart from Malaga. Another enjoyable dinner on board the ship, before our next port of call.

If ever a short visit to a destination benefitted from lots of advance planning, Casablanca is it. I've already mentioned at the beginning of this book, the romantic notions I may have held, and the inescapable associations the city has with the 1942 American movie, starring Humphrey Bogart and Ingrid Bergman.

Our research on Casablanca indicated that it was generally regarded as an unlovely city.

As the *Preziosa* slowly approaches the port area of Casablanca, we are out on our balcony as the sun comes up. The landscape and the fawn-tinged colour of the sky immediately tell you that you are leaving Europe and entering North Africa.

Ahead and to the starboard side, the soft morning light hazily illuminates the 210 metres high minaret of the Hassan II Mosque, facing the Atlantic Ocean from its promontory.

The huge minaret, which is topped by a laser, the light from which is directed towards Mecca, points skywards from behind a collection of less than lovely apartment blocks. In the foreground, the area of the docks immediately in front of us features two grey, military-style vessels.

To the port side at the rear, the heavy industrial area of the docks makes its presence felt. Giant platforms which look like Meccano sets also reach towards the sky, with hundreds of ships' containers forming a carpet around their bases.

The whole view is partially obscured by a grey-brown gritty emission that is arising from a ramshackle building on the dockside. We can taste this metallically-edged grit cloud in the air as much as we can smell it. The morning haze may look romantic, but what it partially obscures is simply heavily industrial.

Neither of us likes going on organised tours, so we have put together an itinerary for the day which suits us. This should allow us to get a flavour of the city, but with minimal hassle, if that were possible.

Those previous visits to North Africa have prepared us for the press of eager, shouting taxi drivers waiting for us when we get to the end of the dock. Although we know where we want to go, they all have different ideas as to where we actually should go, most including a visit to their brother-in-law's souvenir shop, or some similar destination.

We're now used to the fact that maintaining a friendly approach and staying calm in the face of unwanted attention is the way to go. Lots of smiles and polite deflections of the drivers' unsolicited suggestions.

We eventually agree on a price to be taken directly to the massive Hassan II Mosque, the second largest mosque in Africa and the seventh largest in the world. We pay the driver in US Dollars because the Moroccan *Dhiram* is currently a closed currency, so we don't have any.

The $5 cost is well above what any local would pay for a similar taxi journey, but I'm not sure that the concept of being ripped off is really particularly useful, or even valid when one has just stepped off a cruise boat in a relatively poor country.

We are dropped at a convenient point for the taxi driver and we make the longish walk in the strengthening sunshine across a huge flagstoned plaza towards the mosque. The walls of the mosque are made from handcrafted marble by skilled artisans who were drawn from all over Morocco.

A maximum of 25,000 worshippers can be accommodated inside the mosque and 80,000 outside, giving a grand total of 105,000. For no good reason, it occurs to me that this is coincidentally the same attendance as the largest football crowd

I've ever been in, at Hampden Park in the 1960s!

I mention this astounding fact to Fiona. "Fascinating," is her succinct response.

The building, completed in 1993, looks very new from the outside, and the combination of light fawn stone with dark green embellishment is a very attractive one. By now it's hot and squeezing into small areas of shade outside becomes essential.

The view of the mosque and beyond the buildings out towards the sea somehow reminds me of the *Malecon* - the waterfront in Havana, Cuba. Like its Cuban equivalent it is a favourite place for families and teenagers to promenade and congregate.

After the customary confusion, we join the correct queue to buy tickets to allow us to have a timed entry into the building. Inside, the mosque seems improbably vast and largely empty.

All of the materials used in its construction were sourced in Morocco, apart from some Italian white granite columns and 56 glass chandeliers. All of the decoration is of traditional Moroccan design. The building as a whole combines Islamic architecture with more local Moroccan elements.

It references Moorish influences but also presents a modern urban feel, including a discretely hidden, state-of-the-art sound system. It even has an electrically operated closing roof. A bit like Wimbledon.

Part Two of the day's plan is to persuade an ATM to give us some *Dhirams*, which we achieve without too much trouble. After about ten minutes of trying unsuccessfully to hail a taxi, a miracle occurs.

An older driver pulls over to pick us up and it transpires that he actually uses his fare meter. We then take a very cheap 45-minute trip across town to our next destination, Casablanca's *Habous* quarter. This area is a sort of smallish *souk* but without much of the hassle and high-pressure salesmanship, and with less risk of pickpockets.

We have a lovely tagine lunch in a traditional family restaurant, which has a welcome breeze coming in through its windows. We finish with an assortment of delicious local pastries and strong Arabic coffee, whilst being entertained by indefatigable musicians of indeterminate age.

The Moroccan couple sitting next to us appear to be on a date, going by the amount of smiling and laughing going on. The man orders and they are brought an array of food that would probably feed six people. For a couple of days. They eat less than half, but perhaps the main goal is to impress the lady, rather than to satiate their hunger.

We then have a brief shop and manage to buy some nice souvenirs at a reasonable price, without feeling pressurised and annoyed.

Paranoia about missing the cruise boat departure time again ensures that our taxi back to the docks delivers us in plenty of time for dinner on board. All in all, a very enjoyable day, because we planned where we were going to go, what we were going to do and it all went smoothly.

Back aboard the *Preziosa*, we head towards the final stop on our short cruise, Portugal's capital city Lisbon. We are due to make stately headway and to arrive in Lisbon around 7:00am. However, a medical emergency on board means that we have to speed up and so we arrive in Lisbon around midnight.

We can only hope that the poor casualty gets the medical attention they need and that they make a full recovery. The silver lining for us is that we can view our arrival from our balcony, as we enjoyed doing in Malaga and Casablanca.

We pass under the famous *Ponte 25 de Abril* suspension bridge over the River Tagus, floodlit in the darkness, and look over the balcony rail towards Lisbon, with its monuments also brightly illuminated.

Our Airbnb apartment is in the *Cais do Sodre* district of the city, in a newly developed apartment block which was formerly Lisbon's grand General Post Office. Airbnb is so huge in Lisbon that the local government has apparently now banned new licences in large parts of the city.

After getting a few Airbnbs under our belt, a certain type does begin to emerge and repeat. These are spaces which are beautifully designed and carefully furnished and decorated. Very good on the eye and with an instant impact, especially in photographs.

What tends to be lacking is the advantage of anyone ever having actually lived in them, and so they can sometimes prove to be infuriatingly impractical in parts. In this case, the apartment is vast but has only a tiny kitchen area, in which it is not only almost impossible to even make toast and coffee, but it's actually downright dangerous, due to unavoidably close proximity of the water supply with some slightly eccentric-looking electrical appliances.

Lisbon is a beautiful city with a very open and airy feel to it. We do a great deal of walking in the hot sun, visiting the wedding cake-like Jeronimos Monastery in Belem, with a stop to sample some delicious *pastel de nata* in the oldest *pastelaria* in the district, Pasteis de Belem.

We head back down to the beautiful *Padrao dos Descobrimento* monument, to Portugal's explorers through the ages, on the banks of the River Tagus, which ends its 1000km journey from the *Montes Universales* mountains in mid-eastern Spain close to Lisbon.

We stroll still further out along the riverside to the slightly gothic and haunting Tower of Belem, jutting out over the Tagus. As we sit looking out over the river, the MSC *Preziosa* sails past and on out of Lisbon without us. Happily, that was our intention and not a recurrent nightmare becoming reality!

The Portuguese capital is another city which we have visited separately, but this is our first time here together.

On our only full day, we decide that Lisbon is so large and spread out that we'll take the Red Bus city tour, which will allow us to visit other areas we've not seen before. The first circuit takes us up on the famous No. 28 tram route, without the tourist crush.

Also without the risk of expert pickpockets. We go past the Pantheon to the castle.

The idea is to get off at a couple of places, but the driver is obviously behind time. He hares along the narrow old town streets, narrowly missing a succession of pedestrians. He doesn't announce stops and waits only a few seconds at each before moving off. We therefore have to wait till he completes the full tour circuit, and the bus mercifully changes driver. We then get off the bus to enjoy the views and take some photos, second time around.

Fiona has carefully chosen our accommodation so that it is just a few steps from the huge Time Out Market - a massive hanger, now housing a large number of excellent food and drink stalls. Prices are reasonable, the choice of food and drink is excellent, and the atmosphere is buzzing, so we decide to eat there on both nights of our stay. These markets, invented by employees of Time Out magazine, are popping up in a range of cities. They are well worth a visit if they turn out to be as good as Lisbon's version.

Lisbon is a beautiful city which deserves more time than we have. It is booming financially, with a massive tourist trade, but still has very poor, edgy districts cheek by jowl with rapidly developing ones. The city is definitely a great destination for a weekend break, perhaps off-season, if such a time still exists here.

And so our short cruise on the high seas has drawn to a close, appropriately enough in a city which is rightly famous for the exploits of its mariners. The cruise experience has been mostly positive again and it has suitably whetted our appetites to try a longer, and perhaps more exotic, version in due course.

Helpful Hints: Cruise on the MSC Preziosa

Decide what your preferred experience is whilst cruising, in terms of cabin, eating, drinking, and entertainment. It is possible to have an enjoyable cruise experience even if you are not keen on traditional cruise entertainment or dining arrangements.

A cabin near the middle of the ship offers the least chance of rolling movements at sea. Try also to get a cabin away from bars and lifts!

Malaga feels like a lovely, civilised city. The art galleries are interesting and the Alcazaba is worth the climb! A long weekend would be ideal here.

Casablanca requires planning as it is a huge and not all that lovely city. However, it has a number of great things to see. Take some US Dollars with you but try to get to an ATM for Dhirams as soon as you can.

Lisbon is beautiful, buzzing and slightly edgy, depending upon the districts you visit. Keep your valuables close, especially on the trams.

Portugal's capital city is also very big and spread out, so a taking a few days to explore it is ideal. Don't miss the district of Belem with its beautiful monuments, its attractive waterfront and the gothic Belem Tower.

CHAPTER 27: SOL DEL ESTE, MENORCA

A flight from Lisbon to Mahón, via Barcelona, takes us back to the blue and white island, one of our favourite places in the world.

When we go back to somewhere that is as familiar as Menorca - an island that holds a special place in our family's experiences - the temptation is always to re-tread old ground. It's nice to enjoy the nostalgia for when our kids were small, and we used to come on holiday with Fiona's mum, now sadly departed.

It's fantastic to have our own family apartment in Sol del Este, and we could pretty much fill our time visiting beauty spots we are familiar with, and our favourite bars and restaurants.

We do try, however, to seek out and visit a new megalithic archaeological site each time we come here, and to explore new places to walk, as well as new places to eat and drink.

It has been interesting to observe the development of the city of Mahón, from the slightly rough industrial city of the early 1990s - the chemical factory and the cement works are still in evidence - to the increasingly sophisticated and cosmopolitan place it has become. It's also always interesting to compare and contrast the culture we are becoming more and more attuned to, with that back home in Scotland.

On a Saturday night, we catch a taxi into Mahón, and have a couple of drinks in the 1927 *Mercado de Pescados* (fish market), now a bar/café. The bar is lively and buzzing as normal.

Once we've settled down with our drinks, on stools beside one of the barrel tables, I become aware that an unusual scene is developing in front of us at the small wine and beer bar. A chap, probably in his late 20s or early 30s, is standing alone at the bar, talking to the barman. The young man is in floods of tears and is clearly quite distraught. We discreetly conjecture that the cause may be matters of the heart.

The barman talks to him calmly and patiently. A very large black-clad steward is keeping a weather eye on events but makes no move to intervene. The barman and the customer hug, more than once, but the latter continues to be very upset.

"Back home, the bouncer would have manhandled him out of the door by now, and chucked him roughly out on the pavement," observes Fiona quietly.

We move on to another favourite back street bar, *Cristinal y Gradinata*, which seldom sees a tourist. The average age of the bar's clientele is greater, but its eccentric ambience, the delicious range of hot filled rolls, and the red *Portia* wine are excellent. No one here seems distressed, happily.

Two or more hours later, we stroll back down to the *Mercado de Pescados* to try to get a taxi back to Sol del Este. We sit down on a bench in the balmy evening air, to be met with a familiar view. The same guy as earlier is standing outside the iron gates to the bar and is still crying profusely. He intermittently accosts passing strangers for a chat and a hug.

I know it is only one small vignette of life in this city, but here there really does seem to be a bit more of a tolerant attitude to people who are behaving a little differently. Patience and empathy, as opposed to aggression, seem to be the primary responses here.

This chimes well with the ethos of the recently resurrected professional basketball club on the island. Hestia Menorca Basquet tries to pull all the basketball activities on Menorca together, under the banner of seeking to improve mental health, particularly that of young males. The Club's motto *"Una illa, un equip!!"* (One island, one team!!) reflects this sense of togetherness in pursuit of a common purpose.

We manage to take in a match during our stay - once more against Albacete, the same opposition who pipped Menorca by two points in the equivalent fixture we watched last season. This time Menorca's strengthened squad run out winners by eleven points, so things are looking good for a promotion challenge. Even Fiona is beginning to extol the virtues of individual players, and she is also becoming committed to the cause.

To bookend our trip, after our outward flights to Sicily were cancelled due to the British Airways pilots' strike, Vueling inform us that there is a time change in our first flight home, from Mahón to Bilbao. A closer examination illustrates that this is a bit of an understatement: they have brought the flight forward by two days. So now we have three hops home: Mahón - Barcelona - Bilbao - Edinburgh, instead of two.

However, we know that some folk trying to book flights close to the time of departure have discovered that, in the wake of the Thomas Cook debacle, other airlines have hiked their prices up as demand is high. Perhaps we are not so badly off after all.

In addition, Barcelona airport has recently seen disruption during the Catalan nationalist protests, so we'll see what is happening once we get there. Apparently, there have been protest rallies here in Mahón too, but obviously these have not been taking place on days we've been in the city, so we have been blissfully unaware of them.

Spanish flags are again much in evidence in this southeast corner of the island, as they were at the time of the Catalan referendum itself, which led to the political imprisonments that have sparked the latest violence.

So, Retirement Trip Number Two draws near to a close. We felt that Trip Number One in Portugal and Spain had been so good that we couldn't possibly emulate it. However, Trip Number Two has honestly surpassed it for us. Fiona's planning and organisational skills have come up trumps once again, and we have had a wonderful, and at times quite spectacular, trip.

There may have been a few more times on this trip when she wanted to throw me overboard or push me into the crater of a live volcano, but once again we have rubbed along pretty well, on the whole, I think.

We would go back, in the blink of an eye, to Lipari - who wouldn't want to spend some more quality time on a 1950s Italian film set? Also, a return to the unique island of Stromboli would be good - who wouldn't want to live in the shadow of a persistently erupting volcano?

Sicily was certainly an experience, mostly a positive one, though we both agree that it is an island we'd find it difficult to fall in love with. We thoroughly enjoyed Ortygia, and the city of Siracusa in general, to which we'd like to return. Taormina and Ragusa were great towns with spectacular scenery, but one visit will probably suffice. Catania was not that great, and we'd avoid the airport there if at all possible. We'd love to see Mount Etna on a clear day.

The nagging feeling persists that Sicily has so many natural wonders, so many beautiful towns and cities, and as a result has such a burgeoning tourist trade, that it should be somewhere up alongside (the albeit much smaller) Menorca, in terms of its wealth and standard of living. The fact that it is so far short of that, with ropey infrastructure and crumbling public services, and poor people in abundance, indicates that the money that should be addressing those issues is likely being diverted elsewhere.

We finally made it to Portofino, which was almost impossibly picturesque, and implausibly expensive. Again, a single visit will probably do us. We'd like to see a bit more of Genoa, and definitely of the Italian Riviera, which looks spectacular.

Casablanca provided an intriguing, if brief, return to North Africa, but one visit will suffice, whilst Malaga and Lisbon would be great cities for a weekend break, or a little longer stay.

The MSC cruise itself was slightly reminiscent of the curate's egg, really good in parts, and mostly positive, especially our lovely cabin and balcony, and we definitely wouldn't rule out cruising again in the future. The proverbial wild horses could not keep us away from Menorca, though it turns out that Covid-19 can and does, at least for the whole of 2020!

CHAPTER 28: LONG-HAUL TRIPS

Back in those hazily remembered days before our children came along, we managed a few long(ish) haul trips, financed mainly from the bonuses which Fiona gratefully received, whilst she worked in Edinburgh's finance sector.

Kuoni was a favourite tour operator of ours in those days. The company marketed reasonably priced long-haul holidays, which we could just about stretch to afford. Once they had you at your destination, Kuoni tried to entice you onto their quite expensive organised excursions.

So, we reasoned, if we used the trips to get to fairly nice hotels in interesting far-off places via reasonably priced flights, then did local excursions under our own steam, we could just about manage these holidays.

And so we came to visit India, Thailand, Bali, Hong Kong, and Egypt with Kuoni between 1983 and 1989. On one occasion, as we left Hong Kong for our next stop in Bangkok, we read that there had been an attempted coup in the Thai capital.

Two Australian journalists had been shot, one sadly fatally. Newspaper front pages bore distressing images of one of the journalists being dragged away from the scene by his colleagues, leaving a trail of blood along the pavement.

As we are transferred by bus from Bangkok Airport into the city, the Kuoni representative gives us a little talk about the city's attractions. When he asks if there are any questions, a couple of our fellow holiday makers raise fairly innocuous queries, which are readily dealt with.

I can't quite believe that the previous day's coup attempt remains unmentioned, so I raise it. Kuoni's man fixes me with a somewhat impatient look and indicates that this was merely "a little local difficulty". Our holiday will be entirely unaffected by the Thai army having to be called in to quell an incipient revolt.

After 1989, of necessity - family and financial - we pretty much limited ourselves to Europe, including our favourite Greek Island groups and the Balearics. Other than the aforementioned cruise to the Caribbean from New York in 2011, Europe it was - predominantly destinations around the Mediterranean for the next 15 years or so.

Towards the end of my career with the University, I was fortunate enough to be allowed to attend and present at conferences first in Siem Reap, Cambodia, and then at Singapore University.

So long-haul flights beckoned once more, this time in Business Class for possibly the only time in my life!

Cambodia was the venue for the 2016 11th Asia Pacific Biosafety Conference, during which the annual meeting of the Executive of the International Federation of Biosafety Associations (IFBA) - the overarching group whose members comprise all of the world's biological safety and biosecurity organisations - was to be held.

I was invited to present to the Executive regarding my University's online biosafety training programme, which was developing apace to try to help meet the training needs of the international biosafety community. So, I decided to attend the conference and take up the IFBA's kind invitation.

Because I'm flying Business Class with Etihad Airways, a driver and swish car pick me up at my house and take me to Edinburgh Airport, in plenty of time to be at the front of the queue waiting to board at the gate.

When the flight to Siem Reap, via Abu Dhabi and Bangkok, is

announced, I eagerly shuffle forward with my hand luggage. I can see an Etihad flight attendant standing just inside the doorway smiling with a welcoming glass of champagne - *my* glass of champagne. I manage to get one foot on board the plane when an announcement booms out to the effect that there is an issue with the onboard software and so boarding will be delayed.

I am turned around, gazing longingly at my disappearing champagne. The couple of folk before me in the queue, who had got a few steps into the aircraft, are hustled off. If anyone had officially boarded, all the luggage would have had to come off and be matched up with its owners, a situation the airline is understandably keen to avoid.

Still, the delay allows me to sample another unfamiliar luxury - access to the Business Lounge, where an excellent and relaxed breakfast can be consumed, whilst catching up with the newspapers.

Two hours later, the problem is resolved, boarding is resumed, and I am finally united with the waiting champagne. All the better for the wait. Food and service are at a level to which I am not accustomed, and the onboard entertainment is engaging.

"Why has it taken me to the age of 61 to experience this?" I ask myself but then resolve just to enjoy this rare experience as it occurs.

At Bangkok airport, I finally wind my way to my departure flight for the Bangkok Airways flight to Siem Reap. As we fly over the hilly border area between Thailand and Cambodia, the rainforest or jungle (I'm not quite sure which) covered hills poke up through the mist.

The plane is very small and the food is not quite Etihad Business Class standard (in fact, I'm not quite sure what it is).

Siem Reap Airport seems to contain the only rude and unfriendly people in the whole of Cambodia. Or maybe that's just how it seems at the end of a long journey.

Given the way in which the country has been ravaged by

invading forces over the decades - by 2016, over 100 people per year were still being killed by unexploded ordinance from past conflicts, mostly by standing on it - the welcoming nature of the Cambodian people is quite astounding.

I find that warm and friendly as they undoubtedly are, Cambodians do tend towards frankness.

Following a fascinating trek in the temples, in midday temperatures of 104 degrees F, I am greeted warmly as I stagger out of our hired driver's car and pass through the front doors of my hotel.

"Ooh, Mr. Reid. Your face is very red. You are sweating a lot. Are you all right?" This after 30 minutes in a beautifully air-conditioned car on the ride back.

I eschew the smart come back, along the lines of "Really, I felt it was a little chilly today," and settle for stating the obvious - yes, it is rather hot out in the glaring sunshine with 90+ humidity for good measure.

Sensible locals avoid being out in the heat if they possibly can, but I'm afraid mad tourists have to venture forth when they can. It is undoubtedly worth the effort, and a local beer tastes all the better for it.

When the time comes for my presentation, I set off for the tuk-tuk ride to the conference hotel in plenty of time to allow me to locate the meeting room and scout out the audio visuals well before the meeting commences.

Some dodgy directions, no doubt due to the language barrier, unfortunately send me off on a wild goose chase around the hotel's lush and extensive grounds in a large golf cart, just as the morning heats up nicely. The hoped-for calm start to proceedings has evaporated along with the sweat from my brow.

By ten minutes before kick-off, I have been dumped at a rear entrance to the hotel, now more lost than when I started out.

I venture to the nearest entrance, mainly to get out of the heat. I'm immediately greeted by a very friendly and welcoming gentleman, as I approach the serried rows of seats facing a projection screen.

"Good morning, sir! Indian Toilet Conference?" he smiles engagingly.

"No. Sorry. Wrong meeting." I stammer and make a beeline past bewildered-looking participants in what was undoubtedly shaping up to be an interesting and rewarding day in Indian Toilets. Biosafety would undoubtedly be relevant to proceedings. I could have learned a lot.

I emerge into the hotel's main corridor, moments before my meeting is due to start. I stop and stand under an air conditioning outlet in a desperate attempt to cool off and calm down.

Mercifully, at that point, like manna from heaven, a well-known face from the world of Dutch Biosafety, who also happens to be a keen ex-basketballer, appears through the lift doors. We exchange a few words of greeting, then I follow him to the meeting room for the IFBA Executive event.

As we finally reach the door, one of the administrators who is helping to organise the meeting, appears through it looking a little harassed and mildly dishevelled.

"Please excuse my dewy appearance," she mumbles. "The room's aircon has completely broken down, I'm afraid."

And so it comes to pass that, a few moments later I am standing at the front of the meeting room, having been introduced by the IFBA President, delivering my presentation on online biosafety training, with rivulets of sweat running down my back and behind my ears.

This discomfort is not helped by the fact that the room audio system has also failed, leaving me to speak the commentary to a short video section, a second after listening to the commentary previously recorded by one of my colleagues back in Edinburgh. The commentary is playing on the laptop's reedy speaker a few feet to my right. So I try my best to perform like a newsreader on a very low-budget TV channel - words flow in one ear and out of my mouth.

Still, I have the small consolation that everyone else in the room is also physically uncomfortable, as the large free-standing conventional fans, which have been hurriedly assembled, fail to make much impression on the rising temperature and increasing humidity.

As Rabbie Burns once remarked: the best-laid schemes o' mice an' men gang aft a-gley. But Shakespeare's retort would be: all's well that ends well. The people I meet are interested and interesting and the contacts made that day lead to positive spin-off discussions and opportunities over the coming months, as I and my colleagues had hoped.

And several beers that evening are, I feel, richly justified. Just to rehydrate, obviously.

Once the employer-funded working section of the trip is over, Fiona and Kathleen fly all the way out to Siem Reap to join me for a holiday, which is lovely.

One evening, we visit the lovely Siem Reap Raffles Hotel, for cocktails and snacks. We are just settling down on a comfy couch in the attractively opulent surroundings. Just at the moment the waitress brings our orders to the table, my phone rings. The display tells me it is our son Sean, who is at University back home in Stirling.

"Sorry to bother you dad, but I fell in the street and I think I may have a concussion." Even at this distance, I can tell that he is sounding a bit confused and so is quite possibly concussed.

His sister assumes a familiar "What's he done now?" expression. We offer long-distance advice on getting a taxi to Accident and Emergency, but in the end, settle for his assertion that his girlfriend is coming over. She'll stay at his flat and keep him under observation overnight. He seems OK with that.

We return to our cocktails, with much shaking of sibling and parental heads.

Many fascinating temples are visited in the stifling heat, and we have a memorable post-conference holiday, during which our admiration for the people of Cambodia grows and solidifies.

Even the waiter in the hotel cocktail bar, the one with the infectious laugh, who insists on addressing me loudly and enthusiastically each evening: "Ah, Mister Reid - Happy Buddha!" Laughs maniacally.

This is because he is marginally slimmer than me. OK, considerably slimmer. Oh, how everyone laughs - at me, of course.

Still, I do get my own back on the journey home. Business Class for me, with champagne and all the other trimmings, not to mention the ability to stretch out horizontally in my personal cubicle to sleep. I am, however, magnanimous enough to pay Fiona and Kathleen a visit back in Economy, part way through the flight. Unfortunately, I pick a time when they have just managed to drop off to sleep. Ah well.

The next year, 2017, a year before I retired, another such opportunity arose. This time I was invited to speak at a laboratory safety conference held at Singapore University.

Business Class once again with Etihad, with all the advantages of the previous year, but I make the mistake of flying out the day before the conference started, rather than allowing myself an extra day to acclimatise.

By the time I've gained entry to my room in the late afternoon, I am past famished and exhausted. A room service dinner, then off I go to bed to catch up on some sleep, before my presentation in the morning.

Unfortunately, at 3:00 am Singapore time my phone, which is charging on the desk on the other side of the room, shatters my slumber. Fiona is mowing the grass at home and has inadvertently phoned me.

So I spring from my bed, and skid across the carpet, only to meet with her profuse apologies. Only very fitful sleep comes to me after that, as my thoroughly confused biological clock refuses to close down again.

Still, the presentation goes well in the morning, though the Chemistry undergraduate lecture, in which my section of the proceedings is being held, has fixed seats and desk curves suitable in size for Asian and Far Eastern students.

I have to endure the ignominy of a chair being brought especially for me to sit in at the front and wait for my "spot", as fitting into a row of seats is out of the question. Honestly, I am not *that* overweight. The locals are just very slim and petit.

As the previous year, Fiona and Kathleen take the opportunity to join me for a post-conference holiday. We visit lots more temples, though not quite so many as in Cambodia, and have a memorable trip up the Mekong Delta in a canoe, though the river is rather crowded with visitors.

We also make a trip to one of the most bizarre places we've ever visited on any trip abroad - the Ba Na Mountain Resort. The longest cable car system in the world takes us ever higher towards Ba Na, over spectacular scenery including sections of jungle and rain forest, and Da Nang City.

As well as a view of Da Nang, the vista includes Vung Thung Bay, Hai Van Pass, Son Tra Peninsula, My Khe Beach, Marble Mountain, Thu Bon River, and Cu Lao Cham Island.

Sun World Ba Na Hills itself is described as "an exotic theme park with lots of recreational amenities perched on a high mountain (1487m above sea level)". We had consulted reputable guidebooks before leaving home, which assured us that Ba Na offered a beautiful forest walk to a lovely waterfall, as well as a massive white marble Buddha.

The latter is unmissably there and is indeed spectacular. And even fatter and whiter than me. The forest walk appears to have been long swallowed up by the less than tasteful resort development. This is a salutary lesson that sometimes even the most up-to-date editions of top-name guidebooks do not keep up with the times.

The resort is a reproduction of someone's idea of a mediaeval French village, perched atop a Vietnamese mountain. It is absolutely thronged with visitors, many of them Vietnamese, who fill its plentiful bars and restaurants to overflowing. In a nutshell, it is a theme park hater's worst nightmare.

To make matters still more surreal, our visit coincides with the Munich Beer Festival, which is being enthusiastically celebrated. Accordingly, there are a large number of fairly inebriated, apparently local, youths in attendance, some of whom develop an annoying fascination with Kathleen.

After a quick lunch and a walk around, including one German beer each, just to be sociable, we decide enough is enough and head back down in the cable car. Not wishing to put anyone off Ba Na, but it's best to know what you are about to be visiting, rather than being seduced by a memory of past glories.

Another visit that was both disorientating and disturbing, though, in quite different ways to Ba Na Resort, was to the War Remnants Museum in Ho Chi Min City (Saigon). This large and modern building was formerly called The Museum of American War Crimes but has since been diplomatically re-christened.

First opened to the public in 1975 the museum is a shocking reminder of the long and brutal Vietnam War. Captured American military equipment is on display outside the building, including a helicopter, a tank, and fighter aircraft.

America was not alone in visiting atrocities on the Vietnamese people. The French preceded them, and the museum also includes a guillotine and wire cages used to imprison people in cramped, crowded, and generally horrific conditions.

Perhaps the most shocking exhibits are displayed in a single large room. These are an exhibition of graphic photographs of the child victims of Agent Orange, the defoliant chemical spray used by the invading forces during the War. Vietnam's Ministry for Foreign Affairs indicates that around half a million children have been born with birth defects as a result of their parents' exposure. This display is not for the faint of heart. I left the exhibition in tears.

The abiding memory of both Cambodia and Vietnam was of irrepressible peoples who had experienced almost unbelievable hardships during our lifetimes. Yet they came across as apparently forgiving and above all hugely pragmatic. No point in dwelling on past atrocities, however horrific. Much better to look steadfastly forwards and strive for a better life for one's family. Quite humbling in my book.

Both of these trips have whetted the appetite for long-haul travel to exotic locations. On the negative side, they have also reminded us (me in particular) that we are considerably older than we were when we travelled pre-children. The body is less flexible and resilient, and so less tolerant of the physical rigours of hours on a plane and miles covered.

Business Class travel has also spoiled me a bit, but that's out of the question for the future in terms of cost. So, we need to get on and do it as best we can in the health/age window we are currently occupying!

CHAPTER 29: THE WONDER OF TESCO

Elsewhere in this book, I've mentioned the fact that we have taken full advantage of Tesco's voucher reward scheme on several occasions over the years. We've used it to partly or fully pay for flights, cruises, and accommodation where we could.

At the outset I should note that, as well as normally doing regular shopping with Tesco Online, we both have Tesco Bank credit cards. Tesco's voucher reward scheme has altered over the years, in terms of the individual partners who accept Tesco Vouchers, the conversion rate of Voucher value to monetary value in each case, and a variety of other factors.

In general terms, the scheme is not quite as generous as it used to be, but we still happily avail ourselves of its advantages. As recently as our 2021 trip to Menorca we paid for three weeks of secure car parking at Edinburgh Airport in that way.

We have benefited from the scheme many times over the last ten to fifteen years, but three particularly enjoyable instances spring to mind.

Back in 2009, we booked a weekend at one of the most exotic hotels we've ever stayed in - Richard Branson's *Kasbah Tamadot* Hotel near Asni, in the high Atlas Mountains of Morocco.

This multi-award-winning 5* hotel *Kasbah Tamadot* was reportedly identified for purchase by Sir Richard's mum and dad, whilst their son was visiting Morocco with the goal of circumnavigating the globe in a hot air balloon.

The hotel, which is the former home of the antique dealer and interior designer Luciano Tempo, has 28 rooms and suites, each of which has been individually decorated to reflect and complement the beautiful architecture of the building. The rooms and public areas display antiques collected from across the globe.

Kasbah Tamadot's geographical situation is utterly spectacular, nestling as it does in the clear air of the Atlas Mountains. The hotel sits directly across from an ancient Berber village, from which many of the hotel's domestic staff hail. The infinity pool is huge and affords spectacular views of the surrounding countryside.

As we prepared to leave for Morocco, we joked that the Tesco Voucher people would probably be somewhat looked down upon in such a posh establishment. We reckoned we could expect to be seated at a small side table in the dining room, probably beside the toilets, with perhaps a restricted menu appropriate to common folks.

Picked up by car from the airport, we wound our way along increasingly dusty North African roads, edging upwards towards the Atlas, and the small plateau on which *Tamadot* is set.

Once we had settled into our lovely unique and individual room, it was dark outside, and time to go out onto the spacious terrace for dinner.

Contrary to everything we had expected, we were met by the sight of a huge Arabian feast buffet, with not a Tesco-labelled table in sight. The food was marvellous, and the setting spectacular - a dark Arabian night, dining by candlelight in the most atmospheric Moroccan location imaginable. The only negative was that the spectacular views from *Tamadot* could only be hinted at and imagined until the sun came up in the morning.

We had been greeted, when we emerged first onto the terrace for drinks before dinner, by a lovely young woman, who settled us in and chatted away amiably. She told us that she had originally been hired as a massage practitioner within the Virgin organisation, but her wider potential had been spotted, and she now fulfilled the role of assistant manager at *Tamadot*.

She was entirely representative of all of the staff at this top-notch establishment - friendly, relaxed, welcoming, and keen to put guests completely at their ease. None of the stuffiness of some 5* hotels say in London, where staff members appear to have an inflated idea of their own importance.

Most of the other guests of the hotel appeared to be much younger couples, almost exclusively honeymooners. So the pool tended to be quite quiet early in the morning and late in the afternoon.

A second romantic candle-lit dinner on the "ramparts" equalled the previous evening for enjoyment, and at every turn, the hotel grounds and courtyards presented us with fresh beauty and a delightful ambience.

Even with the help of Mr. Tesco, we could only manage to stay at *Tamadot* for a couple of nights, though that was definitely long enough to fall in love with the place, as Richard Branson and his parents must have done.

A couple of years later, we decided to take our first ever proper cruise, accompanied by our (then 16-year-old) son Sean. His big sister and her boyfriend were off exploring the USA and Australia by road, so most unusually the four of us didn't have a family holiday together.

The remaining Three Musketeers flew to New York from London, where we embarked on the Princess of the Caribbean, with a little trepidation as we were not used to taking trips in close proximity to thousands of other holiday makers.

I mentioned to Sean sometime before we left for New York that, as NBA basketball was sadly not available due to a lockout strike, it might be good to see a baseball game in Yankee Stadium.

I got on the internet and managed to secure tickets for the Yankees versus the Milwaukee Brewers the day before our cruise departed from Manhattan.

Showing her normal admirable thoroughness and talent for detailed planning, Fiona managed to discover that there was a "baseball special" boat that sailed up the East River to the Bronx and so to the Yankee Stadium. The launch, run by the Yankees' sponsors, was free to fans.

Unfortunately, en route to New York, Fiona had purchased something in a shop at Gatwick but had managed to leave her credit card in the machine. Naturally, this was the credit card with which she had paid for the baseball tickets, and which the rules clearly stated had to be presented when picking the briefs up at the stadium.

So, Sean and I got ourselves over from our hotel in Brooklyn to South Street Sea Port in time to join the boatload of beer-swilling Yankees fans on a gloriously sunny trip up the east side of Manhattan. This was quite the most spectacular journey to a sporting event that we have ever made.

The mood on board was slightly raucous and beery, but amiable. Happily, there were none of the undertones a football special train would have back in the UK. It certainly beat the Blue Train from Glasgow Central to Mount Florida, for the few Cup Finals we get to attend as Hibs fans.

When we got to the ticket booth at the Yankee Stadium, happily no long and desperate explanation was required, as no mention was made of producing the purchasing card. All that worrying for nothing.

Once the novelty of being in a baseball stadium, clutching a flat European beer at $12 a pop, had worn off, there then followed around four hours of almost complete tedium. One home run was scored, at some point, though I'd already long lost interest by then. The crowd made subdued noises at various junctures but what notable play had been made entirely escaped me.

The spectators were generally the entertainment in themselves. They only became really animated when the possibility arose of individuals appearing on the huge scoreboard. Kiss Cam, Dance Cam, Air Drumming Cam, quite possibly Pick Your Nose Cam. All seemed to provide much more entertainment than anything that happened in the match.

Towards the end, we'd both had enough, so we made our way down onto the concourse and into one of the huge Yankees merchandise stores. It was crowded with fans purchasing Yankees gear. Clearly, this was much preferable to watching the team play.

From memory, the Yankees lost narrowly to the Brewers. Nobody seemed that bothered. No wailing, no booing, and no gnashing of teeth like after a Scottish football defeat. Perhaps we just picked a dull match. Or maybe baseball just isn't our thing.

Our cruise ship carried around 11,000 passengers and was pretty much a state-of-the-art vessel for its time, in 2011. One attractive feature was the top deck basketball court, with which we tempted Sean out of his cabin and away from his electronic games.

A basketball tournament was announced. Sean was by now a much better basketball player than I had ever been and was playing at the National League level in Scotland. I was still playing for fun once a week.

We teamed up with a teenage American girl, with whom we had got talking earlier on deck. The tournament was 3v3 into one basket, on a slightly spongy-surfaced court. We drew an American dad in his late 40s or early 50s and his two early teenage sons. As soon as I saw the dynamic between them, as we warmed up and made ready to play, I knew we could take them.

What? Basketball is always serious, even holiday cruise ship basketball, and we didn't want to get knocked out in the first round, did we?

As the game got underway, my silent predictions were proved right. We started well and went a few points up. The super competitive American dad began to criticise and cajole his sons, to urge them on to greater efforts, he thought. Their team's cohesion started to fall apart.

We had progressed into a fairly comfortable lead over the American combo when he decided to take matters into his own hands. He drove hard to the basket and I jumped vertically - probably a full three inches off the ground - to try to block his shot. I got a firm palm to the ball as it left his hand, and thumped it off the backboard, only to see the ball whirl teasingly around the hoop, before dropping through the net for two points to them.

Much worse than that, however, when I landed on the spongy court surface, I felt something go twang in the outside of my right knee. This is seldom a good thing.

I managed to see out the few remaining moments of the tie, and our wee team successfully progressed into the next round, where a much younger, faster, and more skilful Japanese chap substituted for me, for the rest of Sean's team's stay in the competition.

The next day, I hobbled painfully around the wonderful Puerto Rican rainforest. This was one of the highlights of the whole trip. I had to stop regularly to rest my knee whilst grimacing sheepishly. I never did get a diagnosis for the injury, but it took quite a while to fix itself.

As well as Puerto Rico, we visited Bermuda (lovely) St. Thomas in the American Virgin Islands (less lovely), and Grand Turk. From the latter, we took a trip out across the dazzling azure sea, in a small brightly coloured reggae-blasting boat, to an uninhabited island. There we made the acquaintance of some friendly stingrays.

These amiable, if less than stunningly good-looking, fish were obviously well used to entertaining tourists. The rays allowed themselves to be held up for inspection and used as instruments to massage our shoulders.

Their deadly stingers were proffered to each of us in turn. It was explained that you ensured one year's good luck if you ran your finger along the length of the stinger to its tip, but five years of good luck if you did that with your tongue.

To my family's horror, I did the latter. Superstitious, moi?

The one thing we were firmly warned not to do was to lift or stamp our feet in the water. If one of us stood on a ray, it might well react by firing off its stinger, and woe betides anyone who got in the way of that slim but deadly missile.

Around this time, Sean looked over my shoulder out to sea and emitted a sound that was approximate to "Wey-hey!" with a broad grin beginning to spread across his face. I looked around, expecting perhaps to see a female swimmer emerging from the warm waters of the lagoon, sans bikini top.

Nope. A shark had just slunk into the small bay, obviously wondering what was going on. Now I am not talking about a Great White here: this looked like a Caribbean reef shark, perhaps 6 or 7 feet in length, but it moved disconcertingly swiftly. Once its presence became known to the other people in our party, some degree of consternation ensued.

The most animated of our number was the very small Chinese lady who was standing beside me. When she saw this fine example of *Carcharhinus perezi,* she immediately grabbed my right arm and started babbling.

She also started jumping up and down in a couple of feet or so of water in which we were standing. Standing surrounded by rays complete with their worrying stingers, you will recall.

"Please don't do that!" I said urgently to her, to which she babbled away (to me) unintelligibly and stamped even more enthusiastically. We managed to beat a hasty and disorderly retreat onto the golden sands of the beach. I had to drag the excited lady out of the water by one arm, like a misbehaving child, and disaster was mercifully averted.

That was, however, the end of the afternoon's water-based activities, and we climbed back on the boat to journey back to Grand Turk. The shark had disappeared as quickly as it had arrived in the bay.

Midway through the return trip, I swayed up towards the bow of the boat to stretch my legs and look at the view. I noticed a blue-green tarpaulin. It was almost covering something grey and apparently bleeding. Something around 6 to 7 feet in length.

We couldn't prove it, but we reckoned that the guys who were running the stingray molesting trips had decided to kill two birds (or perhaps one reef shark) with one stone, by removing an unwelcome visitor who might prove bad for business, whilst presumably also achieving a nice wholesale price in a seafood restaurant back on Grand Turk.

All in all, our first ever cruise did whet our appetites for future such journeys, hopefully minus basketball-related accidents. Thanks are due again to Mr. Tesco for a large dollop of assistance with our inaugural foray into cruising!

As the years passed and Tesco's scheme changed towards the slightly less generous, we've tended to use the voucher scheme for limited parts of trips, rather than the whole shebang.

Our first Aeolian Island, the 1950s film set that is Lipari, which kicked off our 2019 trip (see Chapter 21) is one such example.

The trip got off to a great start, thanks partly to the lovely boutique Hotel Borgo Eolie with its friendly staff, lovely pool, and fabulous shuttle bus service.

Thanks to Tesco's linkup with Hotels.com, we managed to pay for the whole week's accommodation on Lipari with the vouchers, which naturally left more funds for the excellent food and the equally good Sicilian red wines and local beers.

Before and since then, various weekend hotel stays, airport car parking and occasionally all-inclusive short holidays, have been added to the list of benefits we have accrued from the Tesco voucher scheme.

We can certainly say that we have taken full advantage of the scheme through the years, and a big thank you is due to Mr. Tesco for his kind assistance!

CHAPTER 30: TOES BACK IN THE WATER

Menorca, September - October 2021

Eighteen months of a mixture of (almost) full and partial isolation from family, friends, and almost all other aspects of "normal" life take their toll.

Even if individuals can steer clear of contracting the dreaded Covid-19 virus itself, and otherwise stay reasonably healthy, physical wellbeing still suffers. Exercise becomes a deliberate act, rather than a mixture of that and incidental exertions. Working in the garden, for those of us fortunate enough to have one, is weather dependent. Other significant health issues need to be addressed, and visits to dentists and hospitals carry their own risks.

Mental health issues are almost inescapable, with the worst probably being felt by people who already experience some degree of isolation, which has become still more acute and even less bearable.

As our thoughts turn tentatively to trying to travel once more, in however limited a fashion, the state of play globally is an overriding factor. The UK's traffic light system brought its unique stresses and strains, which none of us had had to deal with previously. Even once relaxed, the system required unwieldy form filling and other tedious preparations and adds to the costs of travel abroad.

Not only are these definite additional costs sometimes potentially prohibitive in the case of full quarantine requirements on return to the UK, but the very uncertainty of the whole situation added significant stress to any planning.

Indeed, the uncertainty of a fluid scenario, subject to sudden and unpredictable change, understandably acts as a deterrent for many, who decide to stay at home.

It takes us many weeks of indecisiveness before we conclude that the benefits outweigh the risks, in our particular situation. We begin to plan for our first trip abroad since the autumn of 2019.

We delay and delay making any concrete arrangements, partly because we have become almost conditioned to exhibit the isolationist feelings and behaviours engendered by the pandemic, and partly because we don't want to risk losing substantial sums of money if the trip, like so many others, doesn't materialise.

We decide that three weeks staying in our family's small apartment on the quiet(ish) island of Menorca would be just the ticket. Finally, the bullet is bitten and flights and car hire are booked.

The late summer of 2021 has also brought the complications of me requiring two hospital procedures to further address my personal plumbing issues and the recovery periods which were necessary following each one.

So, perhaps predictably, the build-up to us leaving is not the most relaxed. I finish a course of antibiotics for a post-procedure infection only a couple of days before we are due to fly out. Happily, my GP agrees to prescribe a further course of appropriate medication as an insurance policy against another similar infection arising whilst we are away.

A few days before we leave, I manage to slightly tweak my back lifting a full basket of washing to hang out in the garden. On the morning of the day on which we leave the house, I can barely hobble, as lower back pain has set in. Extra back medication and a lot of lying down get me into a state (just) fit enough to travel.

Our neighbour Niall, who had kindly offered to take over on wheelie bin duties in our absence, asks us what time our flight out is.

"4:00 am," I reply, looking rueful as the time approaches and reality begins to set in.

"The airport will be nice and quiet then," he smiles encouragingly.

Very early on the morning of our departure, we join a very long queue for check-in, with Jet2 staff trying to streamline progress as much as possible, to facilitate passage through the new paperwork/electronic jungle imposed by Covid-19 restrictions.

The Security Hall is like a huge rugby scrum, with social distancing non-existent. Fleetingly, it reminds me of the old tradition of The Ba' in Orkney, where great masses of young men try to move a ball past each other through the streets of Kirkwall, to score a victory and ensure the bragging rights for their end of the town till the next contest.

There's a feeling of almost frenzy in the air, as many people are going abroad for the first time since the onset of the pandemic.

The flight has been consolidated, to pick up homeward-bound passengers at Palma, before hopping over to Mahón, then returning to Edinburgh with them. This means that the plane is busy, and some seating confusion ensues. Some people aren't getting the facilities they have planned and paid for.

However, after two years of absence, we eventually relax a bit and welcome back the familiar experiences of air travel. These include shrink-wrapped, limp but scalding, cheese and tomato toasties. Some things never change.

I had anticipated feeling quite emotional when I stepped off the plane at Mahón airport. Being able to travel to Menorca had become something of a fantasy for us, and the other members of our family, during the long months of lockdown.

Instead, I experience only a feeling of unreality, which persists for quite a few days, before we both settle down to being fully present in this most familiar of destinations. It's genuinely hard to believe we are finally here.

During our first week, temperatures hang around the low thirties, so much of life is conducted outdoors in the glorious sunshine. This is hugely welcome for folk like us who have hardly seen the sun for months and is also good for Covid infection control.

It becomes apparent that the vast majority of tourists on the island are from the Spanish mainland. They and the local folk are as courteous and considerate as normal, with people leaving even outdoor restaurant tables to smoke at a distance. Despite a relatively low number of Covid cases on the island, considerate mask wearing is the norm.

On the evening of our first full day, we take a taxi into Mahón. It's Saturday night, and the old 1927 fish market (*Mercado de Pescados*) is teeming with younger revellers. The atmosphere is slightly raucous but positive and friendly.

We decide to give the crowds a miss, although the *Mercado's* bar/pinxchos restaurant is a favourite of ours. We spot a new restaurant opposite, a tapas place with a Far Eastern slant, so we take an outside table.

We've both become familiar with the Track and Trace QR codes, in bars and restaurants back home. There is a large QR code on one corner of our table. I go to scan the code into my iPhone.

"Don't do that!" hisses Fiona. "We don't want to get pinged and have to isolate when we've just arrived here."

"It's OK," I retort. "I'm just going to scan it for appearance's sake, but I'll not complete an online notification."

"Don't do it at all! We don't want to take any chance of being pinged," says she.

As we are arguing, a young waitress approaches and asks us if we'd like to order. I ask her for menus. She indicates that by scanning each table's QR code diners can link to the current menu. We ask for a few more minutes to decide.

When she leaves again, we sheepishly scan the code and peruse this evening's choices. As we are to discover, this practice is now the norm in virtually every café and restaurant we visit during our three weeks on the island.

It's no doubt great to be paperless, but sometimes the link doesn't work properly, and a lot of scrolling down is also required when we want to surreptitiously consult the English language version of a menu if we're not sure what a dish is in Spanish. However, nobody tracks and traces you afterwards.

Well, one has to learn sometime. We act like old pros with regard to QR codes from then on, and I try to converse and order in Spanish as much as possible, to justify the lockdown hours I've spent back home on Duolingo.

In one restaurant, under new management, on the *Molls de Llevant*, the road which runs along Mahón's gorgeous marina, we decide to take an unusual step and order an organic white wine. It goes by the name of *Pim Pam*, and we are assured that it is "unique and unusual."

By the time we are halfway down the bottle, the contents of our glasses have begun to visually resemble one of my recent urine samples. I'm not sure which liquid would have tasted better. We should have known by the name.

We meet up with an old friend who has moved permanently to Menorca, on her own, a couple of months before the pandemic was declared. She describes the feelings of isolation she has experienced.

For a considerable period of local lockdown, she was only allowed to walk around the swimming pool, in the internal gardens of her apartment complex in Cal'an Porter. Any thoughts of integrating and making new friends inevitably went by the wayside.

Another acquaintance in Sol del Este, whose wife had recently passed away, had been restricted during lockdown to shopping only at the closest small supermarket. Individual shoppers were allowed a daily visit lasting no more than fifteen minutes.

The local police were empowered to examine supermarket till receipts to check that no one overstayed their allotted time slot. Fines were levied on anyone who was found to have transgressed.

He had had to make an arrangement to pick up "essential" weekly veterinary supplies for his dog in Mahón, in order to allow him the opportunity to visit a much larger supermarket in the city.

Living just up the road from our apartment in Sol del Este, he had been turned back home by police whilst walking along the almost deserted cliffs close to his apartment. He reckoned only the company of his faithful canine companion had kept him sane.

So even on a tranquil and beautiful island like Menorca, the effects of the pandemic on people's lives, and particularly on the state of their health, have been profound.

For us, just managing to be here has been hugely positive for our well-being. Although restrictions had eased somewhat back in Scotland, there's a real feeling of freedom to move and breathe here. We enjoy immensely the feeling of being considerably more normal, but still feeling quite safe, on a day-to-day basis, for the first time in a long time.

The fact that the weather is so balmy, whilst a wet autumn is turning towards winter back home, definitely helps.

The pandemic hit Spain early and hard. Some businesses have disappeared, but the ones which were already pretty successful look to have flourished.

Excellent new bars and restaurants are popping up, and some which had become a bit run down and tired have been taken over and rejuvenated by new management. The lovely art deco-style American Bar in the centre of Mahón has benefitted from a particularly welcome revamp.

Happily, the island's basketball club has survived, though we won't be able to take in a home match during our visit, as the LEB Plata fixture list for this part of the season is against us.

As I've mentioned previously, the Club's ethos within the Hestia Fundacion is to highlight and seek to help improve mental health issues, particularly relating to young men on the island. One suspects that these issues have grown considerably in volume over the last 18 months.

One hugely positive development has taken place on one of the islands out in Mahón Harbour, a ten-minute boat ride from the city. *Isla del Rey* (or *Illa del Rei*, in Menorquin) was home to a military hospital, on and off, from 1711 until the 1830s.

In 1974, the Town Council offered the island to the Spanish Government so that a government-run Parador could be built there. This project did not come to fruition. The hospital buildings and the internal garden were declared a National Historical and Artistic Monument in 1979.

In 1985, the island became the property of the Town Council of Mahón. One proposal was to build a 5-star hotel on the island. Again, no concrete movement transpired on this.

The Association of Friends of the Hospital Island was formed in 2004, and in 2005 the Association was converted into a Foundation (*Fundación Hospital de la Isla del Rey*). The Foundation's objectives are to ensure the protection and development of *Isla del Rey*, and to promote and organise events relating to the island.

Many volunteer hours have been spent painstakingly restoring the hospital, pharmacy, chapel, and grounds for the education and pleasure of visitors to the island.

The Foundation has worked with Hauser and Wirth on the conservation and development of run-down outbuildings on *Isla del Rey* which have been repurposed as a stunning art gallery. It is an exhibition and teaching space that integrates beautifully with the surrounding scenery, flora, and fauna of the island.

The development, which opened to the public in July 2021, also incorporates a sculpture trail, which includes one superbly expressive, flowing black sculpture by Miro which stands in the garden created by the award-winning garden designer Piet Oudolf.

The gallery, sculpture trail, and gardens are complemented by an excellent restaurant *La Cantina*, run by our local winery, *Bodegas de Binifadet*, which is an old favourite of ours, with vineyards ten minutes up the road from our apartment towards the town of San Luis.

We eat sheltered by a grove of trees, looking out across the water towards Cala Llonga, buffeted by a chilly wind off the water, which doesn't impair our enjoyment of an excellent *Menu del Dia*. Weather conditions do, however, negate the desire to linger, and we're glad to get back into the warm sunshine once more, in the interior of the island.

The only downside we could see in this marvellous project is the fearsomely expensive gift shop!

Hopefully, the easily accessible gallery and its accessories will be a big hit with both local people and visitors, and the project will contribute positively to Menorca's ever-growing reputation for conservation and the arts, as well as to the local economy.

On our second weekend, we treat ourselves to dinner, bed and breakfast in the Barceló Hamilton hotel, down by the harbour side in the small former garrison town of Es Castell. This wee holiday within a holiday is paid for by the wonderful resource that is Tesco Vouchers, as highlighted in Chapter Twenty Nine.

The hotel is designed to look like a cruise ship sailing out of Mahón harbour, and our superior room (thanks Mr, Tesco!) affords us fantastic panoramic views of the mouth of the world's second largest natural harbour. Worth waking up to watch the sunrise, from the comfort of our huge double bed, naturally.

The hotel's Blue Sky Bar, with its cool (in both senses of the word) rooftop jacuzzis and cabanas and wonderful views, is officially closed. We take drinks up from the downstairs bar so we can enjoy the view in the late afternoon sunshine.

Another bar we visit four or five times in the course of our stay is *Som Si,* another very cool little open-air establishment that is perched on the narrow road which runs up from the promontory at Binidali, on the southeast coast.

The German proprietors were also a little cool when we visited previously, but they seem to be warming to us as we pop into their bar more often. The small seating area boasts a fabulous view out over the cliffs, and the deep blue waters of the inlet at Binidali beach. The beach itself is also small, but very popular when the sun is shining.

We sit lingering over *cafés con leche* and mineral water *con gas.* Lovely, airy jazz emanates from *Som Si's* crystal clear sound system and drifts out towards the cliffs. The bright sunshine

WHAT'S THE TIME IN CASABLANCA?

sparkles blindingly off the surface of the Mediterranean. Tapas and desserts are chalked on a board, should peckishness strike.

The only slight blip in this idyllic interlude comes when we are sitting next to a table occupied by a German family. The adults are chatting away animatedly. Their very small girl is very bored. She plays under the table close to their relatively old Labrador, whose panting indicates that he or she is feeling the heat.

The little girl discovers a small container of pointed wooden cocktail sticks on the table. She amuses herself by seeing what happens when she sticks their sharp points in and around the old Labrador's eyes. The dog is understandably unimpressed but shows admirable restraint and indulges the child for a while, before upping and moving to a safer location.

We wince repeatedly and exchange looks. Should we say something? In the end, customary British reserve and my fading knowledge of schoolboy German, together with the need to avoid a scene at all costs, win out. We hope that the doggie has a better time for the rest of his or her holiday. And that the little girl doesn't grow into a sadistic serial killer.

The ambient temperatures, particularly during our first week on the island, are considerably higher than those we normally experience when we visit slightly later in the year. This encourages us into La Gardenia's large and lovely, but entirely unheated, outdoor swimming pool.

We get chatting with an English lady from the apartment opposite ours. Earlier in the day, I'd noticed her and her husband walking up the stairs to the entrance, their shorts revealing huge and angry red insect bites on the backs of their legs.

Our neighbour mentions that they had both been particularly afflicted by mosquito bites during this trip. We sympathise, having experienced similar, though not quite so florid, bites in the past.

"Yes. The problem is often those nasty Zebra mosquitoes," empathises Fiona. "The little buggers get you during the day, as well as after dark. It's really difficult to keep your exposed skin topped up with insect repellent at all times."

When we are alone again, I gently inform her that the little buggers in question are called Tiger mosquitoes.

"Well, they've all got stripes haven't they?" comes the irrefutable reply.

Three weeks on the island pass remarkably quickly and, even after so many visits over the years, there are still things we don't get around to doing. The Quarries of *S'Hostal* (better known as *Lithica*), and the *Cova de s'Aigua*, both in the region of Ciutadella on the west side of the island, will have to wait until our next trip.

We have to admit we've been good to ourselves on this first post-lockdown trip abroad - lots of nice bars and restaurants - but there is undoubtedly a sort of demob feel about the holiday. We'll definitely be more frugal next time. Maybe.

Just getting here has been decidedly good for the soul and the feelings of near normality have been stronger here than at home in Scotland. However a long Scottish winter is in prospect, with uncertainty about Christmas arrangements as the pandemic doesn't look to be ending any time soon.

We are both now Covid boosted and influenza jabbed, so a controlled return to the world is still the name of the game. Life will continue to be subject to more overt balanced risk assessments than it was in the previous decade.

The full return of global travel as we knew it is probably quite some time away, but there are still great places to head for in the current situation, albeit always keeping an eye on sensible measures to safeguard one's personal safety and health.

So, now we are back in the saddle, maybe a cheeky wee trip further south in the depressing months of January and February of 2022? We shall see - fingers firmly crossed!

CHAPTER 31: EDINBURGH TO MAHÓN

September - October 2022

As it turns out, no winter trip materialises. What does materialise is the Omicron variant of Covid-19, which rears its spiky head, causing another UK lockdown to be put in place. Christmas 2021 celebrations are muted and limited.

So, as we move into 2022, we start to plan the third long trip since my retirement in 2018, feeling that it's time to be optimistic once more. Once the latest restrictions are lifted, we need to take steps to get back in the saddle, metaphorically speaking.

Retirement Trips Numbers 1 and 2 have both exceeded our hopes and expectations. We decide that Trip Number 3 should be made up of a mixture of new places we want to see, including destinations we feel we had unadvisedly missed out on back in 1980, and places we would like to revisit now we have more time and a bit more money.

Covid-19 put paid to our plans to travel to South America in 2020, as it put paid to everyone else's travel plans. The idea was to fly to Buenos Aires and stay in both Argentina and Uruguay, then board an MSC transposition cruise back, stopping in three locations in Brazil, then a few other interesting ports of call on the way up through the Atlantic and into the Mediterranean on the way home.

The cruise industry has been very hard hit by the pandemic, and we all remember the news reports of cruise boats, filled with sick people, being refused entry to various ports across the world.

In order to keep its customers on board (if you'll pardon the pun) MSC Cruises keep in touch and keep offering us incentives to swap to a different cruise. During 2020 and 2021, as the pandemic develops worldwide, we are offered a further four replacement cruises in turn by the Company. On each occasion, negotiations ensue, after which the replacement cruise is duly accepted. In each instance, the new cruise is then inevitably cancelled due to the pandemic.

Finally, in the latter part of 2021, we opt for an eleven-night cruise in the Eastern Mediterranean which we accept, and which miraculously (it feels like) goes ahead! All the negotiations with MSC during 2020 and 2021 mean that the final cost of the cruise is very reasonable, to say the least.

As the MSC Fantasia will leave from Trieste in Italy, we decide to plan a trip that brackets those eleven nights with travels by sea, rail, and occasionally air, in the Adriatic, mainland Italy, and to some Mediterranean islands in the latter part of the trip. As usual, there is much discussion as Retirement Trip Number Three starts to form in our minds.

The plan this time around is to fly with Ryanair from Edinburgh, via Brussels South Charleroi, to Pula on the Adriatic coast of Croatia, from where we'll get a car to the lovely town of Rovinj. We stay just over a week in Rovinj, in a hotel on a small island opposite the fishing port.

We then make another car journey up the coast to Trieste, on the border between Italy and Slovenia, where we stay for a single night, before boarding our cruise ship the MSC Fantasia, to cruise around in the Eastern Mediterranean.

The first port of call is the city of Zadar on Croatia's Dalmatian coast. We then head to Bari on the southeast coast of Italy, from where we hope to visit the ancient cave city of Matera, which features in the latest 007 movie.

Then we head east to the port of Piraeus for Athens, forty-two years since our last visit to the Greek capital. From Piraeus, we sail on to Turkey, and Izmir, from where we hope to fulfil a long-held ambition by visiting the huge Roman site at Ephesus, one of the wonders of the ancient world.

Back on board for the short trip up the coast of Turkey to Istanbul, for a two-day stay where Europe meets Asia. Back to Greece in the shape of the Ionian island of Corfu, where we look forward to renewing our acquaintance with the elegant and buzzing Corfu Town.

Then we sail back up Italy's Adriatic coast to Trieste, to conclude our cruise with MSC.

From Trieste, we take to the train once more, for the relatively short trip to Venice, again our first visit back to that magical place since 1980. We'll stay in an apartment in a converted palazzo with a small garden overlooking the Grand Canal for four nights, before moving on to Verona. The city of Romeo and Juliet is one we misguidedly missed out on visiting on our trip across Europe to Egypt, way back in 1980.

We stay four nights in Verona, then we catch the second flight of our trip which takes us to Sardinia for five nights. Then we take a ferry to Corsica and stay five nights in Bonifacio in the south of the island. These are two islands that are new to both of us, and which we've both wanted to visit for some time.

From Corsica we fly to Bordeaux and then on to Mahón, for ten days in our family's apartment in Sol del Este, Menorca to wind up the trip.

By our initial reckoning, the seven-week trip allows us to visit six different countries along the way - Croatia, Italy, Greece, Turkey, France, and Spain. In practice, six becomes 7!

CHAPTER 32: ROVINJ

Our four-stage journey starts in Edinburgh at 7:15am, takes us by Ryanair to Brussels South Charleroi Airport, then a second flight to Pula in Croatia, followed by a car transfer from Pula to Rovinj on the Dalmatian Coast, and finally by small boat to the Island Hotel Katarina, where we arrive at about 11:00pm.

The inbound plane for our second leg is late arriving at South Charleroi, and we wait for it to land in an area by our Gate which is packed with young people, who look as though they may be heading for a music festival in Croatia. This does not auger well as we try to remain Covid-free as far as possible, so we keep our facemasks firmly on and try to sit as apart as possible from the animated throng of (mainly) teenagers.

The sight of these kids reminds us that our son Sean went to a similar festival in Croatia a couple of years ago. His mates went out a week ahead of him, and he then flew out to join them. Unfortunately, the travel arrangements were left in the hands of a friend who didn't realise that there are two civil airports in the country whose names begin with the letter "Z" (Zadar and Zagreb). He booked Sean a flight to the wrong one, leaving him to trek halfway across Croatia by bus to the festival site. He got there, and they all met up in the end, and a good time was apparently had by all.

Ryanair's crew achieves a remarkably quick turnaround, and we leave for Pula just about on time. An hour and a half in the car, then time for a quick beer on the Rovinj waterfront before the final leg by boat to our island hotel.

We head along for breakfast in the morning. According to

a large sign in the vast dining room, Island Hotel Katarina identifies as the second-best hotel in Rovinj. Presumably, it reckoned it was the best until its futuristic, super environmentally friendly, very trendy sister hotel the Grand Park opened quite recently across on the mainland.

Indeed, it was a TV series – "Amazing Hotels: Life Beyond the Lobby", in which Giles Coren and Monica Galetti travel the globe, visiting and working in some of the world's most incredible hotels - which featured the Grand Park and the town of Rovinj itself, which first put the location on our radar.

We waste an hour or so of our first morning waiting for the safe in our room to be repaired. It's an essential item, as we need to store our laptops and my camera and lenses securely. The technician comes along with his "stupid tourists" face on and instructs me to watch as he demonstrates how to operate the electronic locking and opening system.

I look over his shoulder, suppressing a smirk, as he repeatedly fails to get it to work. He eventually leaves and promises to return with a new safe. After he has fitted that one, we fill it with our valuables and successfully lock it. I then realise that he hasn't bolted the safe to the wardrobe shelf, so it can just be lifted out and removed, for a thief to open later at their leisure.

We are about to take this up with the hotel reception when we further realise that bolting the new safe to the shelf would be pointless, as the small shelf itself lifts easily out of the wardrobe, with the safe on top. At that point we give up.

The weather forecast is decidedly depressing for pretty much our whole time here, but happily it's largely wrong. Violent thunderstorms during two nights sandwich a single day on which it is too rainy and windy to go anywhere outside. Happily (for me) that coincides with Hibs v Aberdeen on Hibs TV, which I watch upstairs in the hotel's grand salle, so I don't miss an enjoyable win.

Other days are all lovely and sunny, which allows us to laze about and swim in the unusual and huge hotel pool - a picture of faded elegance rather than a shiny modern space - and to explore the pleasingly picturesque Old Town across the water.

The hotel owns the whole island, which has areas of pebbly beach, pine forest, and paved walks as well as the classy Batimar snack bar down by the waterfront. We come to understand that the reason Batimar is so good is that the sunbathing area, with the very posh loungers beside it, accommodates well-heeled clients from the Grand Park, who pay to be ferried over in a slick launch. They can then lounge, drink and eat whilst staring back across the bay at their own grand hotel, which doesn't have a similar waterfront area. Everyone to their own, I guess.

Our first foray into Rovinj in the evening sees us strike lucky. We decide to be smart and circumnavigate the queue outside the Stella di Mare restaurant, by sitting in the bar next door and asking a friendly waiter to tell us when a table for two might become free. As he is just about to do so, the owner of the restaurant appears and gives the waiter a bit of a telling-off for accommodating us in this fashion. He then surmises that we have probably heard the interchange, so he comes across to the bar, takes Fiona by the hand, and leads her through the whole restaurant to the best table in the place, down by the floodlit waterside.

I follow in madam's wake and, when we get to our table, I suggest to the owner that he might like to keep Fiona, in return for a bottle of his best Malbec and some of his delicious-looking pannacotta. He fails to respond. Well, I have to admit, the pannacotta turns out to be really excellent.

The food, the place, and the welcome are so good that we return more than once during our eight-day stay. One of the friendly waiters tells us that in a previous storm, two tables were swept into the water. He and a colleague jumped in to retrieve them, and he was promptly carried away by the waves. Despite the fact that he says he is a rudimentary swimmer, he washed up right across the bay on Katarina Island, where our hotel is, and had to spend the night on a bench on the small pier. Some degree of embellishment perhaps, but a good story all the same.

On one evening when thunderstorms are consistently predicted and the wind blows up a choppy crossing to the town, we decide to stay on the island and sample the hotel's dinner buffet. Fiona is immediately scandalised by the tiny measure in her glass of red wine, rapidly followed by the pedestrian nature of the food and the Day-Glo ice cream. The huge dining room is sparsely populated. Now we know why.

She appears close to exploding and witheringly declares the cheese to be "pointless". Her mood is not improved by her having added to her dental woes by chipping a tooth on a sherbet fruit earlier in the day. Naturally, the thunderstorm fails to materialise. She declares the evening "a waste of calories" and we retire to our room. Even if Adriatic waves are colossal and lifeboats have been deployed, we'll be taking the boat to town for subsequent dinners.

We explore the Old Town by climbing up the winding, impressively cobbled narrow streets until we reach the large church which dominates the highest point - the Basilica of St. Euphemia.

The relics of the Saint are preserved in an, originally Roman, sarcophagus from the 6th Century AD. Legend has it that two local fishermen, caught in a storm, pray for salvation. Their prayers are answered, and they awake near Rovinj's shore, in time to see a shining white light hovering over an object that sinks into the sea. A pious local widow makes a plan to retrieve the object, with the help of some sturdy oxen.

The oxen pull the sarcophagus from the water and up the mountain. A religious sceptic falls unconscious and has a vision that the sarcophagus contains the bones of the Saint. The holy relics are then apparently stolen by the Genoese, then nicked off them by the Venetians, before the Saint comes to her current resting place in the Basilica, in the 14th Century.

The interior of the church is hugely ornate and very muggy, so we don't hang about indoors too long - there is a good breeze outside that takes the edge off the heat and humidity.

Officially bilingual, Rovinj (Croat) or Rovigno (Italian) strikes us as being a wee bit like Mykonos Town in Greece's Cycladic Island group a few decades ago, perhaps with a little bit of Lipari, in the Aeolian Islands, thrown in. Rovinj has very quaint streets, expensive shops, and every available space is being converted into a bar or a restaurant. The town is still lovely and laid back, however, with a wide range of ages and styles of tourist winding their way about.

Other than eating and drinking, and climbing up to the church, there's not a whole lot to do in the town, and we take a long boat trip up to the Lim Fjord, which is a pretty stretch of green/blue water passing between attractively wooded banks. It seems to be a popular and highly touted trip, but if you've been to Norway or even our own Scottish Highlands, it may seem a little unspectacular. It's a nice, chilled way to spend an afternoon, however, with friendly staff dispensing copious free drinks along the way.

In the middle of our eight-day stay, the temperature drops overnight from a hot and muggy 29 degrees to a cool and breezy 13. The relaxed time we've been having is soon impinged on somewhat by the need to each do a Covid test, supervised via video link to a London laboratory, and get a certificate issued to us, as part of the requirements to board our cruise ship in Trieste in a couple of days.

We have tried to be Covid careful - if we don't get on the ship, we have an eleven-day hole in the middle of our trip. This possibility only fully surfaced in our collective consciousness around a week before we left Edinburgh, so it is a tense half hour in our hotel room until both tests come up negative and we are emailed our certificates for embarkation!

Helpful Hints: Rovinj
Visit the Dalmation coast of Croatia - why on earth did it take us so

WHAT'S THE TIME IN CASABLANCA?

long to come here?

If you stay in Rovinj, consider one of the island hotels, a few minutes away from the town by boat. If you stay at the Island Hotel Katerina, only opt for the evening buffet in case of hurricane conditions.

Boat trips from Rovinj are lovely, though the Lim Fjord one is perhaps less spectacular than it is marketed.

Sample the restaurants in the atmospheric Old Town, rather than the more immediately obvious ones down by the harbourside.

CHAPTER 33: TRIESTE

We (I really mean Fiona) habitually plan(s) our trips quite meticulously. We leave Edinburgh thinking that we will be visiting six countries in the course of our seven-week trip - Croatia (twice), Italy (three times), Greece (twice), Turkey (twice), France, and Spain.

So, we are a bit surprised when it transpires that in practice that will actually be seven countries. We hadn't realised that the big toe of Slovenia pokes out between Croatia and Italy so the road from Rovinj to Trieste necessitates us passing through border control into Slovenia and getting an entry stamp on our passports.

We have the unexpected pleasure of a 30-minute drive up Slovenian hillsides and down into beautiful Slovenian valleys, before passing along the highway with a fantastic view of the Bay of Trieste on our left. This short advert for Slovenia makes it look very attractive for a future visit, before we pass seamlessly into Italy. Because Slovenia and Italy are both Schengen Group nations there's no need for a border control point between them.

The car transfer delivers us to a narrow side street in Trieste, and the front door of the former palazzo that houses our super swish minimalist and stylish apartment. We already wish we were staying here for more than one night.

We sally forth with a small map and the directions of the helpful receptionist at the Palazzo Talenti. It proves to be just a 10-minute walk through the Piazza St. Antoni, down the Via Rossini, and over the bridge straddling the Canal Grande, to the Piazza del Borsa.

On through the busy pavement cafes and into the hugely

impressive main square, the Piazza del Unita d'Italia. The square and the waterfront remind us a little of Lisbon, both locations emphasising the impressive seafaring history of the two cities.

The grandeur of the vast Piazza is a little spoiled by the presence of a small encampment of white gazebos, which are set up for political meetings - it seems to be election time. We walk on through the grand Piazza to the waterfront, only a stone's throw from the cruise terminal from which we'll leave tomorrow. We arrive at the superbly executed sculpture of two women sewing. At first, I thought this beautiful and moving piece of public art commemorated the skills of the city's seamstresses.

I've since learned that it in fact represents the women of Trieste waiting for their menfolk to come home from war. They keep busy with their sewing to keep their hands and minds occupied, as they wait and worry. Poignantly, decades pass and these two ladies are still waiting.

We stroll back the way we have come and decide to stop for a coffee at the only cafe we can see that is not completely full outside. I ask Fiona what kind of coffee she wants.

"Well they really frown upon people ordering a cappuccino in the afternoon, don't they?" says she.

The waiter approaches, exuding machismo.

"What kind coffee you like lady?"

"A cappuccino please." I'm thinking: she is doing this deliberately.

The waiter fixes her with a look that seriously would be appropriate to her just having mortally insulted his grannie. He turns to me in disgust.

"I'd like an Americano please." This proves to be too much for him. He starts to rant about coffee made with water, with milk on the side, not being the Italian way.

"OK - how about a double espresso with a little milk on the side?"

This triggers a lecture on the need for tourists to learn how to drink the appropriate coffee, in the correct manner, at the proper

193

time of day. It goes on for some time, as he plays to the gallery of other clients of the cafe. We sit impassively until he runs out of steam. He stomps off in high dudgeon to bring us who knows what.

Whilst he is away, we decide not to get annoyed, as would be our norm, but to gently bait him further. On his return, he slaps down a cappuccino and a double espresso with some milk.

I say to him, in the most drippingly sarcastic voice I can muster:

"I really want to apologise for offending your coffee-making sensibilities due to my ignorance. We are Scottish and we have no idea how to make coffee properly. You must get so sick of stupid ignorant tourists coming to your cafe and giving you money."

Instead of sending him over the edge, he smiles, claps me on the shoulder, and suddenly he's my best mate. It dawns on me that this obnoxious person actually thinks that I *am* sincerely apologising to him. As opposed to eyeing up the nearest metal chair leg with the notion of introducing it to his rectum.

He slopes off, clearly content that he has suitably educated two foreign ignoramuses. We drink our weak, lukewarm coffees and leave. We forget to leave a tip.

Dinner by the Canal Grande in the evening is much more enjoyable, in a long street on the side of the Canal which is full of hospitable restaurants with friendly staff. The evening is cool, but the canal-side restaurants and the general atmosphere are buzzing and the welcome is warm.

After dinner, we wind our way back to the apartment. As we are about to cross to the Palazzo Talenti entrance, we become aware of a hooded youth who is lurking suspiciously and who appears to be eyeing Fiona's bag. Or perhaps he is just an assassin sent by the barista at the cafe. We scuttle quickly into our highly secure apartment building.

In the morning, our final views of Trieste include the spectacular Piazza del Unita d'Italia and the rest of the city spread out around the bay, from the vantage point of our cruise boat berth.

Single-night stopovers can often just afford snapshots of places you wouldn't necessarily want to be. Trieste, however, is well worth a visit as a destination in its own right. As with any seaport, it has its rough edges, but it is also unexpectedly (to us, at any rate) elegant and quite beautiful.

And the final view of the port heralds eleven nights on a lovely cruise ship, on the high seas (well hopefully not too high) stopping off at interesting and exotic destinations along the way!

Helpful Hints: Trieste

The city is much more than just a stopover destination. The beautiful older parts are readily walkable and well worth the effort.

Take an intensive course in Italian coffee drinking habits and be prepared to have your credentials rigorously examined before you can hope to be served.

The rows of restaurants down the side of the Canal Grande are a lovely dinner spot.

CHAPTER 34: ZADAR

After a slightly chaotic embarkation process, including the successful presentation of our Covid certification, we get to our well-appointed cabin and begin to orientate ourselves on the MSC Fantasia.

In due course, we set sail from Trieste. As previously mentioned, we got there from Croatia via Slovenia, and our first stop is Zadar in, er, Croatia. Zadar is apparently the oldest continuously habited Croatian city. It boasts the ruins of a huge and attractive Roman Forum and some lovely churches from later eras.

Zadar's premier claim to fame, however, is that it also boasts a very large organ. What's unique about this organ is that its pipes terminate in the side of the sea wall. The waves from the Adriatic Sea change the pressure of the air contained in these organ pipes, which emerge at the other end as barely noticeable holes in the long modern paved promenade.

The sea then plays an erratic, atonic symphony which lots of visitors happily sit and listen to, and which is at the same time strangely haunting and rather comforting. When a boat goes by, the pitch of the notes changes, and the music speeds up, which adds a bit of variety to the aural experience. The knowledge that this is a natural effect of the sea, displayed through a man-made instrument, adds to the enjoyment.

The long waterfront also features the Monument to the Sun, a kind of glass disco floor, which at night flashes multi-coloured lights using the energy it has stored from the sun's rays during the day.

The Monument is in the form of a glass disc, 22 metres in

diameter, which is made up of 300 glass plates that are flush with the surface of the waterfront promenade. This main disc represents the sun, which is surrounded by smaller discs representing the planets of the solar system, and which are proportionate in size. Photovoltaic solar modules with lighting elements lie below the surface of each individual glass plate, and these produce a light show from the stored energy after dark.

We are there in the morning and afternoon, so obviously we don't see the Monument to the Sun in action. Shame. Another shame is that when you build something artistic, inventive, and beautiful as a public installation, attempts will inevitably be made to break it.

Damage, including cracks on solar modules, has occurred on several occasions. The largest disc, the sun, has suffered the most with twelve modules damaged, and so have the planets Jupiter and Saturn. The cracks were apparently caused by a 3500 kg pickup truck driving over the discs. Unidentified objects have caused damage to a further six modules, and in 2019 a young man apparently took it into his head to smash a number of modules with a hammer, causing almost Euros 100,000 worth of damage.

The City of Zadar has now implemented 24-hour physical supervision plus surveillance cameras. It's difficult to get inside the head of someone who wants to carry out such wanton acts of destruction, but it's a mindset problem that extends well beyond the boundaries of Zadar and Croatia.

The city has known a bewildering succession of owners through the centuries. As recently as the early 1990s, Zadar was under siege from Serbian forces, and attacks on the city continued until the end of the Croatian War of Independence in 1995.

Zadar features lots of attractive and intact or restored old architecture spanning a variety of eras, side by side with the brutalist buildings dating from its communist bloc past. The Roman Forum is a case in point - one entire side of the space the restored ruins occupy is flanked by the blocky concrete presence of the archaeological museum.

Zadar has one final claim to fame - the city is the hometown of Croatia's greatest-ever footballer, the midfield maestro that is Luca Modrić. At the age of 37, Modrić is still successfully plying his trade in Spain's La Liga with the mighty Real Madrid, as well as being a standout as captain of the Croatian national team at the Qatar World Cup.

Helpful Hints: Zadar

Unless you want to make a pilgrimage to the birthplace of Luca Modric, Zadar probably only merits a couple of days stay, though on our day trip we didn't have the opportunity to explore possible excursions from the city.

The sea organ area is busy on a good day, but it's really quite a hauntingly beautiful instrument. Staying over will also allow for a visit to the nearby Monument to the Sun after dark, when it is operating.

A walk further along the promenade to the Roman Forum and the Old Town is interesting and rewarding.

CHAPTER 35: MATERA

Stop number two brings us back to Italy, specifically to the port of Bari, in the region of Puglia in Southern Italy. From Bari, we have booked a bus trip to visit Matera, the ancient city of former cave dwellings.

Matera featured in the James Bond movie "*No Time to Die*" which was the twenty fifth film in the Bond anthology, and Daniel Craig's final fling as 007.

I am only aware of the city because of the movie, though Fiona has accumulated more detailed background knowledge. After the evacuation of the population in 1952, the Sassi (Italian for "stones") di Matera lay abandoned until the 1980s.

However, Matera has since undergone something of a renaissance. Some of the cave dwellings have now been converted into boutique hotels, restaurants, small museums, and craft workshops. In 2017, the University of Siena estimated that 25% of the former family housing in the Sassi was available to rent on Airbnb. Matera was designated European Capital of Culture in 2019.

Leaving the cruise terminal in Bari by bus we travel through some fairly desolate looking industrial estates, some of which have what appear to be abandoned apartment blocks incongruously planted in the middle of them. There is an air of depression about the parts of the city we see, and on the road to Matera. It looks like Bari and its environs have not recovered from the 2008 financial crash, with the prospect of another recession on the way.

The road trip affords us brief views of a number of attractive Trulli houses - the dry-stone built dwellings with their distinctive conical roofs which are emblematic of the region of Puglia. Trulli apparently date back as far as the 14th Century, enjoying the height of their popularity in the 15th Century. As well as family dwellings, these unusually shaped buildings were also constructed as temporary field shelters and storehouses by small landowners or agricultural labourers.

The Trulli look as though they may stand the test of time better than some of the much more modern, now derelict, buildings that we pass on the outskirts of Bari.

At one point, we happen upon a car in flames on the opposite carriageway, the accident attended by all of the emergency services. Such events always give you a jolt as they flash by on the highway, and we can only hope that the occupants got out in as unscathed a state as possible.

On a relatively deserted section of the carriageway, we come upon an isolated shack-like house, teetering beside the road, in front of which a number of young women parade in their bright and attention-grabbing underwear. They jump up and down with apparent enthusiasm, waving and blowing kisses to the passing drivers. I am indebted to Fiona for the detail on the last observation, as I naturally avert my eyes.

The structure seems to have an entrance at one gable end and an exit for clients at the other. Not quite a drive through, but I'm sure you get the idea. The air of desperation in the tableau is in keeping with generally depressed vibe in what we've seen of the region so far.

An hour or so on the bus takes us to Matera. The ancient quarter known as the Sassi di Matera is a crowded and haphazard complex of former cave dwellings, which were carved into an ancient river canyon. We read that the Sassi has apparently been occupied through time by the Romans, Longobards, Byzantines, Saracens, Swabians, Angevins, Aragonese, and Bourbons.

By the late 1800s, Matera's dwellings had become noted for crushing and intractable poverty, terrible sanitation, poor working conditions, and rampant disease. The Sassi was known as the Shame of Italy. As I mentioned earlier, the dwellings were evacuated by order of the Italian government in 1952, and the remaining population was relocated to modern housing. The houses, for example had no running water, other than rainwater collected by a funnel shaped opening at roof level, which then fed into a downpipe, which in turn fed water into the dwelling by gravity.

Some inhabitants were keen to go, in order to live and bring up their families in a more modern and civilised environment. Some no doubt fought to stay in their family homes, unsuccessfully in the end.

Matera is the only stop at which we book a guided tour, mainly because we are led to believe that this is the only way we can enter the area! When we arrive at the ticket office, at the top of the slope down in to the Sassi, it becomes apparent that this is not the case, as individual visitors are clearly purchasing tickets and entering the site under their own steam.

We are rapidly reminded why we never go on guided tours. The guide routinely speaks a few words of English, then indulges in a ten-minute soliloquy in Italian complete with jokes and audience interaction. He then repeats what he'd said in English previously, but slightly louder. Any other nationalities are ignored. At one point he vehemently describes events surrounding a forced eviction from the property we are standing in front of, targeting his comments at the non-Italian members of the group as if no other community has suffered similar events. Perhaps someone should fill him in on the Highland Clearances in 18th and 19th Century Scotland.

We learn nothing we didn't already know from guidebooks and become increasingly ratty. Eventually, we abandon our guide as our group waits to join other groups to view the interior of the hot, cramped Covid trap that is the tourist example of a typical dwelling house. We make the long climb back up the hill to the main square of Matera.

We sit down in two cafes for a much need drink and snack but are ignored in both. We leave and end up in a 24-hour food and drinks vending facility, which we finally persuade to give us some sustenance after practically having to iron our banknotes before the machines accept them. We repair to consume our meagre repast by the fountain in the main square, only to be deafened by a man on a stage speaking in an impassioned manner into a microphone. It is election time in Italy.

We return to the bus grizzling and make the return trip to Bari, and back to the cruise ship. It has, however, been a lesson re-learned!

Helpful Hints: Matera

Unless you know of a good tour guide, we'd suggest just paying for individual entry to the Sassi di Matera, and taking a good guide book with you.

Good sensible footwear definitely helps make the visit more comfortable - some of the paved slopes are slippery underfoot.

If you are particularly interested in the Sassi de Matera, it is possible to stay overnight within its boundaries, in an Air BnB or a boutique hotel.

CHAPTER 36: ATHENS

One thing that strikes us on this longer cruise with its multiple stops is the weird feeling of being in Italy one day, Greece the next and Turkey the day after. We are "parachuted" into these amazing locations one after the other, equipped with a smattering of phrases in a different language, sometimes a wad of a different currency, and always encountering different kinds of people, customs, and atmospheres.

Our last visit to Athens was in 1980 for a single night stopover, followed by two weeks of island hopping, then a week back in the Greek capital. Our memories of the city then are of chaotic traffic, heat and smog, together with wonderful sightseeing, including a visit to the Acropolis and various other sites of antiquity.

Not surprisingly, perhaps, we have decided against a guided tour in Athens on this occasion. A shuttle bus takes us up from the vast port of Pireus to the old district of the Plaka, both of which we last visited 42 years ago.

The MSC representative in charge of making sure the right numbers of people get on and off the bus is English, though she lives in Athens and speaks with a Greek accent. She greets us warmly in a Southern English accent, as she confesses to us privately that she prefers British visitors. She is certifiably insane.

Once we are all on the bus, she informs us that she is not a tour guide, though she tries to be helpful by pointing out points of interest on the thirty minute bus route, in English with a strong Greek accent, and also in Italian. This incurs a complaint from a Spanish gentleman up the front, who is unhappy that she doesn't speak Spanish.

She could deal with this diplomatically, by simply re-stating that she is not a tour guide and apologising for her lack of Spanish, hopefully translated for her by someone who speaks both languages. Instead, she gets into a running verbal battle with the man, which carries on for the duration of the drive up to the Plaka, and indeed resumes on the way back some hours later.

It's with some relief that we get off the bus and head into the historic district of the Plaka to wander about on our own. We've discussed the possibility that we might re-visit the Acropolis, but that would take up all of the time we have available, so we decide to spend our time here in a more leisurely fashion.

We are assured that since our last visit the Plaka has been fully pedestrianised, and so it has, apart from the cars, delivery vans and motorcycles. However, the area still has that inimitable chilled feel special to Greece and it is lovely to be back on Greek soil, for the first time since a family holiday in Cephalonia back in 2009.

The ambient temperature is high and so our wandering is punctuated by stops for coffee, great baklava, and lunch in a traditional taverna. Souvlaki and a Greek salad, with a Mythos beer, roll back the years. I mention to the owner of the taverna (Mr. Zorba?) that we cannot get Greek salad as good as this back home in Scotland.

"The ground is different here," he observes, and ambles off to glare at the jam-packed modern cafe across the road.

The Plaka, located in the shadow of the Acropolis, is the oldest district of Athens. Although it sounds like a bit of a cliché, the area is often referred to as being like a village within the vast metropolis that forms the capital city.

Back in the day it was the night club centre of Athens, and that's how I dimly recall it. However, the city authorities closed many of the clubs down by virtue of introducing a ban on amplified music. The district then quietened down, both literally in terms of the decibel count, and metaphorically as rowdy and undesirable elements moved on to other locations.

We wander around the cobbled streets of the Plaka, remembering what is was like to be here, when Fiona and I were aged 21 and 25 respectively. There were undoubtedly lots of advantages to being at that youthful stage, but at least now we can afford to stop for lunch and order a main course each, rather than one between the two of us.

The *drachma* has long passed into history, but the credit card has handily been invented. I suspect that in 1980 we both preferred the Plaka the way it was then, but in 2022 we'd both opt for the way it is now.

The streets don't honestly look familiar - I seem to recall that we were only in the Plaka in the evenings previously - but the smells and sounds do transport us back in time. Swathes of glorious purple bougainvillea spill out over walls and the clear Greek light seems not to be filtered through air pollution this time around.

We happen across a beautifully reconstructed 17th Century *hammam* (Turkish Baths) in a back street, which looks like it could be functioning today. The Bath House of the Winds is apparently the only intact public bath building in Athens, and is a rare relic of the city's Ottoman period.

The attendants usher us in with no charge, but then follow us around as if we are going to steal a half-ton font or a hole in the ground toilet. Or maybe they have had problems previously with graffiti artists. The district is busy this Sunday afternoon, but few people seem to have strayed as far as this fascinating building.

We walk back towards the bus stop at the Arch of Hadrian, glancing up side streets to see the perimeter walls of the Acropolis site towering above. Our short time on the first of our two stops on Greek soil is fast running out, but we've really enjoyed having a few hours under our own steam, just pottering about where our fancy takes us.

Back on the bus for episode two of the MSC rep vs. the Spanish Gentleman, as the former reminds the entire bus of how rude she feels the latter has been to her. Not quite fisticuffs, but there's still time for things to develop further before we reach the port of Piraeus, and the sanctuary of the cruise ship once more.

Helpful Hints: Athens

Athens is vast and very busy, so if your time here (like ours) is limited, forward planning is essential. A longer stay is probably more rewarding, indeed it's essential if it is your first visit to the city - there's a lot to see.

The Plaka, 2022 version, on a clear and sunny day, is a lovely place to amble around, and it has an ample provision of appealing refreshment stops.

*The Bath House of the Winds is located at **Kyrristou 8, Plaka, Athina 105 56, Greece** (Phone: +30 21 0324 4340). The baths are open to the public each day from 08:30-15:30. Closed all day Tuesday.*

CHAPTER 37: IZMIR (EPHESUS)

Back in 1987, Fiona was still working in the financial sector, and we had planned a three-week trip, from Brindisi in Italy by ferry to Turkey, to visit Bodrum, Kusadasi and Istanbul. A day at the huge site of Ephesus, one of the Wonders of the Ancient World (originally seven but lists increasingly seem to vary!) was to be the highlight of the trip.

The outline itinerary was finalised, but Fiona decided that she didn't want to carry on in the finance industry. She opted instead to set up her own high street retail business, in a complete change of career path. Financial considerations dictated that we had to postpone our visit to Turkey. A cheapie week with friends in Chania on the northern coast of Crete substituted - it turned out to be a lot of fun!

I was fortunate enough to make a work-related trip to Istanbul in 2011, which definitely gave me a taste of that great city. However, Fiona's first trip to Turkish soil, and our long-awaited time at Ephesus, has had to wait the small matter of thirty-five years.

As we approach the port of Izmir from the sea, the sun is rising. It casts a lovely golden glow across the waterfront and the various districts of the city which rise up the gently sloping surrounding hillsides. Sunrise on any city tends to show it at its most attractive. As the day gets lighter, Izmir looks less and less prepossessing.

We have to take quite a long bus trip from the cruise ship

terminal to Ephesus. The road up from the port onto the motorway to Ephesus confirms the view that Izmir doesn't really look like a tourist trap.

As we approach the site (again no guided tour required!) we discuss how we'll spend the 2.5 hours we have signed up for on the MSC Ephesus tour before the bus brings us back to the ship. A short way from way from Ephesus, the charming young man who is today's bus monitor - he doesn't speak Spanish either but seems to be forgiven - tells us that we shall have an hour on the site and then perhaps we'll be taken for a little shopping.

Fiona immediately objects forcefully from our seats well back in the bus, saying that we've signed up for 2.5 hours at Ephesus and definitely no shopping - we've been caught out with that one before. A bossy woman a few rows up, who I think is German, has apparently decided that she runs the bus. She has already had the general air conditioning turned off because she is too cold.

She now decides that Fiona cannot understand what the Turkish guide is saying. She starts to try to explain, slowly in English, the information that he has just imparted. She is fixed with a glare that would reduce most recipients to stone and a roared "I'M NOT SPEAKING TO YOU!!" Sensibly the woman regains her seat and faces the front.

The scene has now begun to resemble a cross between Monty Python and Faulty Towers. Once we leave the bus, the argument continues loudly at the entrance to the site and the MSC guide tries to dissuade the ticket office from selling us anything but the most simple ticket, on the grounds that our visit will take too long.

We have carefully researched in advance what we want to see, so we ignore him and buy extra tickets for that area - the recently excavated Roman Terrace Houses. The ticket office staff sensibly decide to stay out of the debate, and just take our offered money.

Eventually, we are grudgingly awarded 1.5 hours on site, so we whizz round in high dudgeon, great heat and, at times, concerningly slippery underfoot conditions. Ephesus is undoubtedly a hugely impressive site, with some fantastically well preserved and restored areas. The Roman amphitheatre is a highlight, as is the spectacular skeletal facade of the Library of Celsus.

The Library, constructed in the 2nd Century AD, was named after the city's former Roman governor, and was one of the Roman Empire's architectural gems. It once contained over 12,000 scrolls, but today only the impressive facade remains as evidence of Ephesus' importance as a seat of scholarship in Roman times.

No less impressive, however, are the recently explored Terrace Houses. These partially restored luxury villas are located on a steepish slope, and they give tantalising glimpses of the life of well-to-do families during the Roman period. The six villas on three terraces lie on the lower end of Bulbul Mountain. They contain beautifully restored decoration, including wall murals and floor mosaics, which we would have hated to have missed.

The area is currently covered with tasteful protective roofing, and sturdy stairways and transparent walkways afford a variety of views down onto the living areas. Their ancient inhabitants enjoyed a sophisticated heating system, which involved clay pipes installed beneath floors and behind walls, which carried hot air through the dwellings, and the houses had hot and cold water.

The sheer size of the Ephesus site is astonishing, and excavations are still progressing. What today reminds us both is that a part-day stop from a cruise boat is not necessarily the best way to see something you are very keen to visit - going under your own steam for as long as you need is infinitely preferable.

Back on the bus for the return trip to Izmir, shopping seems to have fallen by the wayside. We hope that our bossy fellow traveller was looking forward to it.

Just before the bus leaves to return to the cruise ship, a young couple with a baby get on and walk past us to the rear of the bus.

I recognise them, as we were standing close to them in the queue to disembark from the ship, earlier in the day. They both appear to have heavy colds.

As we drive back along the motorway towards Izmir, I seem to develop an annoying cough, which persists on and off for the rest of the journey. Must be the wonky old air conditioning system on the coach, I think to myself, as Fiona passes me a Polo mint to try to shut me up.

Helpful Hints: Ephesus

Allow enough time to see the vast site of Ephesus properly; 2-3 hours would be our suggestion.

Don't omit the Roman Terrace Houses! These reconstructed villas are one of the most interesting areas of the site.

You may be treated to a fairly short acting and dance performance that echoes classical Greece, as you approach the broad avenue along which you leave the Ephesus site.

CHAPTER 38: ISTANBUL

As we sail into the vast and vibrant city of Istanbul in the morning, past the Blue Mosque complex, the Hagia Sofia Grand Mosque, and the Topkapi Palace, we are anticipating that the next two days will inevitably be tiring and full of hassles, but hopefully well worth the effort!

Although I spent a few days here for work back in 2011, it's Fiona's keenly anticipated first visit. My memories of trying to get around this vast city are of hour-long taxi rides, incredible traffic jams, heat, crowds and frustration. So we decide to do it differently, by utilising the city's impressive sounding tram system. At least I know roughly where the main sites we want to visit are located - we just have to find them!

We dock at the huge new Galataport cruise terminal and get organised to disembark as soon as possible. Galataport is at one end of the European side of the city, and we want to go to the other end of the Asian side, to the district of Sultanahmet, where I stayed on my previous visit. We can see it directly across the water of the Golden Horn, but we need to get a tram pass to enable us to take the quickest way through Istanbul's fearsome road traffic, across the Galata Bridge, and back around to Sultanahmet.

A long walk through the corridors of the Galataport takes us through a brand new café/restaurant development and out to the nearest tram stop. Fiona is tasked with obtaining a two-day tram pass and loading enough Turkish Lira on it for our visit.

There is a predictable scrum of bodies around the ticket machines, but two helpful guys are assisting people to pay for their passes and equip themselves with the Istanbul equivalent of London's Oyster Card. One guides Fiona through buying the pass and loading it up, then his mate asks for 150TL for the card itself, which should cost 50TL.

Yup, they are just likely lads running a scam, so she firmly requests all her money back, which is promptly returned, as they move on to the next potential victim. A very helpful local lady then kindly gives us her old card, and we progress to a satisfactory conclusion, at one fifth of the cost. Welcome to Istanbul!

The tram takes us quickly and efficiently to where we want to be, in about a tenth of the time some of my taxi journeys took back in 2011. My previous visit does help though, as we know roughly where to get off to visit the spectacular Cisterna Basilica, which is the largest of several hundred underground cisterns that historically supplied the city with water. Our pre-bought museums pass allows us to stroll slightly self-consciously past a queue of literally hundreds waiting to gain entry to the Cisterna and walk right in - well planned Fiona!

The Cisterna now features multi-coloured floodlighting, and static and kinetic sculptures, in the pools between the seemingly endless rows of huge vertical columns which recede into the distance. A different surprising effect - some ancient, some modern - lies around every corner of the walkway.

The overall effect is quite magical and other-worldly, and the unique atmosphere is enhanced by the drippingly high humidity. We are both bathed in sweat, and feeling a little under the weather, but we assure ourselves that it is unavoidable given the environment we are in.

We spend our day in Istanbul doing exactly what we want to do, at the pace we want to do it. We stop for coffees, wonderful baklava with an ice cream centre, a simple Turkish lunch in the Green Corner Café and just for rest stops, instead of being constrained by an organised tour itinerary.

We come upon a building which I'm certain was not open when I last visited the city - the Mausoleum of Sultan Ahmed I, which is part of the architectural complex of the Blue Mosque (also known as the Sultanahmet Mosque). The Mosque and the mausoleum were designed by the same architect, Sedefkar Mehmed Agha.

The Mausoleum is a monumental building with a domed roof, a square layout, and marble lined facades. Inside are the sarcophagus of the Sultan himself, and thirty-six other tombs of important figures from the days of the Ottoman Empire. The sarcophagi are colourful and ornate, and the small versions for children are poignant.

The interior of the Mausoleum is decorated with amazingly colourful tiles, and the whole effect is quite exquisitely beautiful. Somewhere we hadn't planned on visiting but well worth taking the time to do so.

In the late afternoon we take a very cheap but very long Bosphorus Tour on quite a basic boat, the latter part of which comes after night has fallen. This is a great way to sample both geographical sides of the city. Drinks are dispensed at regular intervals and the cool of the breeze on the water as the evening darkens is very welcome. We return to the European side, and a short tram trip back to the Galataport terminal, in time for a late dinner followed by an exhausted sleep.

Next morning, we are still exhibiting all the symptoms of a heavy head cold. We press on and return to Sultanahmet to visit the famous Blue Mosque. We know from our earlier research that most of the complex is closed due to renovations, but we join the scrum to remove our shoes and enter the bits that are open.

The only section of the Mosque which turns out to be accessible is the Women's Prayer Room, so we end up in the daft situation of getting into a small and really quite uninteresting area, whilst impinging unnecessarily on the ladies' attempts at prayer and contemplation. Allowing visitors into the Mosque when so little of this amazing building is open feels like a bit of a con.

We decide against joining the huge lines out in the square waiting to enter the massive Hagia Sophia mosque, directly opposite the Blue Mosque, and instead content ourselves with admiring its rather odd construction from the outside.

Behind Hagia Sophia, the Topkapi Palace, including the Harem, is spectacular, but so full of tour groups that it is also frustrating and irritating in equal measure. So many of the world's great attractions now seem to be seriously overcrowded, but I guess we can't complain as we are part of the problem. The Palace is almost overpoweringly large, colourful and incredibly ornate. This being my second visit, I begin to feel that it is perhaps a bit on the ostentatious side and that one or two of the palaces we've visited in Spain and Morocco are actually more attractive. However, no trip to Istanbul is complete without a visit to Topkapi, and it is well worth the effort.

An abiding memory of our two days in Istanbul is that of alighting from the tram at the stop for Sultanahmet and walking down towards the park between the two great mosques, just as the muezzin begin their call to mid-morning prayer. The loud echo of the call and response chant/song ringing between the Blue Mosque and Hagia Sofia is hauntingly beautiful, and it reminds us that we really are quite a long way from home, in Asia.

Our time in the city turns out to be much more relaxed than any of the other shore stops on the cruise so far, and much more chilled than I had anticipated after my last visit.

Mind you, that first visit had included a one-hour address in person by Turkey's President Tayyip Erdogan, in a secure auditorium full of tv cameras and ringed by soldiers with sub-machine guns, me completely losing it with a taxi driver and being turfed out of the cab who knows where on the Asian shore, and then also having the misfortune (though nothing comparing to that of the casualty) to be within 20 feet of a serious workplace accident in the grounds of my hotel.

Helpful Hints: Istanbul

Mentally prepare for the attentions of scam artists and other hassles. We suggest not accepting the services of a guide, particularly in Sultanahmet, if they approach you unbidden.

Check opening times and the best times to visit major attractions to avoid crowds. Check particularly the Blue Mosque and Hagia Sofia Grand Mosque in case major refurbishment works are likely to limit the areas you will be able to access.

Buy tickets for major attractions online in advance where possible, to avoid queueing unnecessarily - the Cisterna is a case in point.

Expect Topkapi Palace to be teeming with visitors, so allow plenty of time for your visit. Go to the far limits of the site for a wonderful view out to sea.

Try to use the tram system, which is modern and efficient, if inevitably crowded. Avoid using taxis wherever possible.

Turkish baklava is fabulous - especially the variety with ice cream, along with pistachio nuts, in the middle!

CHAPTER 39: CORFU

A day at sea, and a day in bed in our cabin for Fiona.

My cold bug seems to be improving, but hers is at its worst and she feels pretty rough. We have a quiet day admiring the sea, and order room service in the evening. We curse our luck at having caught colds on the cruise ship, but the environment is one which is notorious for encouraging bugs to spread successfully.

Mask wearing amongst the crew shows 100% compliance, but masks amongst the passengers are few and far between. We wear ours whenever we are moving about the ship, and on other modes of transport such as buses, but we remove our face coverings when eating, drinking etc. on board.

We can't recall all that much about our only previous visit to the lovely island of Corfu, one of Greece's Ionian group of islands. It was a very cheapie week back in 1986, so inexpensive that when we got on the plane we didn't know which area of the island or which resort we'd be staying in. I seem to recall that the price of the holiday, including flights and hotel, was £29 each - cheap even at mid-1980s prices!

Some familiar landmarks loom into view as the MSC Fantasia slides slowly into port at Corfu Town. The Old and New Forts, and the red and white clock tower, are familiar features of the skyline, which is currently partially obscured by low lying clouds.

The bus ride up from the waterfront to the Old Town predictably doesn't show Corfu's most attractive side. There is a bit of an air of depression and dereliction on the way, but the town itself is as attractive as we remember it and the streets are humming with visitors.

Corfu has a strong British connection. Following the Battle of Waterloo, and the Treaty of Paris in 1815, the Ionian Islands became a Protectorate of the United Kingdom. This lasted until 1864, when the Treaty of London led to the transfer of sovereignty of the Islands to Greece. As many of you will know, Corfu was indeed the birthplace of the late Duke of Edinburgh, where he was born Prince Philip of Greece and Denmark.

I had the pleasure of meeting Prince Philip, who was at that time Chancellor of the University, when I was invited to attend a reception for long serving staff at the University of Edinburgh, to mark my twenty-five years in post. When the Duke of Edinburgh first entered the large hall in which we were gathered, he was directed to our small group of three staff members and their spouses.

The Duke peered suspiciously into my face, and said "So what do you do?" I indicated that I attempted to organise occupational health and safety for all of the University's campuses.

"Gawd help us!" was Prince Philip's succinct response, as he moved on to speak to my colleague beside me. It was difficult to take issue with his astute assessment.

Corfu Town's Venetian style buildings reflect its strategic importance in times gone by. The beautiful French style colonnaded pedestrian avenue the *Liston* (from the Venetian) was constructed under French rule between 1807-1814, as a very effective copy of Paris's Rue de Rivoli.

We wander up a side street, which is festooned with colourful flowers, and have lunch in a traditional taverna. The lovely setting enhances our enjoyment of an excellent veal *stifado*, accompanied by a Greek salad, washed down by a very cold Mythos beer served in a frosted glass.

The lovely food and surroundings are slightly detracted from by the odd behaviour of the waiter, who insists on posing for a photo with a middle-aged lady at the next table. In a slightly creepy fashion, he then hugs and kisses her as she and her husband make to leave after paying their bill.

She looks a mixture of pleased and embarrassed by the attention. Her husband looks distinctly unimpressed. The same waiter then brings us our bill and promptly demands a tip for his service, even as my hand is moving towards him holding a 5 Euro note, which I then feel like withdrawing but sheepishly don't.

It is a profound relief that he doesn't attempt to say goodbye to Fiona in a similar fashion, as I can confidently predict what her tip would be.

Whilst in the city, we decide to call in at a pharmacy to get some much-needed cold remedies. The first pharmacy features a rotund and moustachioed chap, who appears to be playing tag behind the counter with a small girl, presumably a relative. He does not appear to noticeably welcome our custom.

Our Greek vocabulary is practically non-existent, so we try to haltingly indicate what we are looking for, showing him an empty cold medication packet. We add that it should not contain ibuprofen, on my account.

He ignores us and chucks an ibuprofen-containing product on the counter, whilst continuing with his game of tag. The little girl is a bit over-excited, and she doesn't really seem to belong behind a pharmacy counter.

We repeat the "no ibuprofen" request. He drops a second pack of something unrecognisable on the counter and loses any slight interest in us he may have had. We pay and leave, feeling a bit doubtful about our purchase.

We stop for a seat in the shade and Google the product the man has sold us. It becomes apparent that it would not be suitable to take with one or more of the prescription medicines that I use on a long-term basis. So much for our fully qualified pharmacist, or maybe it was just the result of a language problem.

So, it's on to pharmacy number two, where we spend about half an hour, as the hugely conscientious female pharmacist practically conducts a PhD research project. Without any prompting from us, she searches the Web and ensures that she takes every possible interaction and side effect into account, before selling us something completely different. However, we do feel a lot better about taking it.

This small (we thought) task accomplished, the rest of the afternoon sees us mooching around town, with coffee and ice cream stops, soaking up the nostalgia of being back on a Greek Island. We mustn't leave it so long again.

Helpful Hints: Corfu Town

Make sure you take a stroll along the Liston - this French style pedestrian street is an architectural gem.

In good weather, the main streets of the town are very crowded, but you can readily slip off into much quieter side streets for a refreshment stop.

You can visit both the Old Fortress of Corfu and the New Venetian Fortress - both are close to the town centre. Check the Web for opening hours for both - these can vary depending upon the time of year.

CHAPTER 40: VENICE

After disembarking from the MSC Fantasia for the final time, in Trieste we join the chaotic scenes in the ferry terminal car park. Buses, taxis, and cars arrive, with little or no sign of traffic control, and no queuing system. He or she who speaks Italian appears to get a taxi, we don't.

We arrive at one cab we think we have hailed, but another couple looms up too. The taxi driver looks studiedly bored and declares himself to be "indifferent" as to whom he takes as passengers. While we are speaking with him, the other couple shoves their luggage in the boot and that clinches the deal.

Fiona has the bright idea of crossing the main road to the large and very posh Savoia Hotel. We stayed for a couple of nights in its sister hotel in Genoa in 2019, which gives us a quite unjustified feeling of connection - like we are valued regular clients who will be welcome at any of the group's upmarket establishments at any time.

We install ourselves in the lobby bar where we order coffee and encounter the red and white uniformed Trieste football team (currently playing in Italy's Serie C) who are in the hotel for a pre-match meeting and meal. They and their coaches lounge about on the expensive furniture, the players (who for the most part look very youthful) glued to their phones until they are ushered into a meeting room, no doubt to discuss the tactics relevant to ensuring that today's opponents go home empty handed.

After a little while we feel that we have blended in with the furniture, so I go to Reception and ask them to call us a taxi to the railway station. It arrives almost immediately, and a polite driver takes us at a reasonable cost to where we want to go - problem solved.

A comfortable high speed train journey from Trieste drops us at Venice Mestre, where we alight just as we did back in 1980, using our Transalpino tickets. We get into a tiny lift on our arrival platform, with just enough room for the two of us and our suitcases. A small and excitable Italian lady insists that there is room for one more, and promptly dumps her case heavily on my left foot. That's a blackened big toenail in prospect for a few weeks - thank you madam!

A local train then conveys us across the lagoon to Venice Santa Lucia. We walk out of the exit marked "Grand Canal" to meet with the same incredible and unique city scene as we encountered open-mouthed 42 years ago.

First task is to buy a couple of week passes for the *vaporetti* - the city's waterborne equivalent of buses. That accomplished, Fiona scans her pass and hands me mine as she walks through the electronic barrier onto the pontoon. The little flappy gates remain open after her. I hesitate, then try to follow her, whereupon they swing sharply shut and hit me in the family jewels. Welcome to Venice!

Two stops up the Grand Canal (one for each aching testicle) and we alight at the pier for our apartment, which is in a former *palazzo*, right on the Grand Canal. It also has that most prized of asset of a Venice property, a small garden with a terrace and a stone balustrade overlooking the canal. Traffic, from gondolas to ambulances, never stops.

We are shown into the apartment and first impressions are a bit iffy. The curtains are closed, and it is quite dark and confusingly laid out. The furniture and the artwork on the walls turn out to be in keeping with an historic Venetian residence, and a little on the gaudy side. It also smells a bit like an old people's home. And that's before we have settled in. Everything in Venice is damp, for obvious reasons, but once we get used to our surroundings, we begin to fully appreciate how good they are - especially the location!

One de-merit, however, is that the small kitchen features a responsive hob, just like *Casa das Flores* in Madeira where we stayed with Kathleen and Sean some ten years ago, and just like our otherwise wonderful apartment in El Puerto de Santa Maria in 2018. As with our previous experiences, this kitchen contains a range of metal vessels, including the familiar Italian style espresso maker, to which the hob will not respond. We eat in only once and it is a fraught experience.

However, each morning we have the wonderful privilege of breakfast on the terrace overlooking the busy Grand Canal. I suggest that to come out with a drink in the early evening would also be really nice, but that we might have a problem with the mosquito population so close to the water. Fiona mentions that the guest book contains a note that the size of the rats which come out to play on the terrace as night falls is disconcerting. We decide against it.

The narrow streets around our front door are liberally festooned with rat boxes, but happily we don't actually clap eyes on a rat during our stay. Apparently clapping loudly as one walks up the echoing alleyways is a good way of getting the rats to scuttle off before you reach them.

Our first full day is glorious weather-wise. We get on a *vaporetto* to travel a few stops down the Grand Canal, but it is so lovely that we decide to gradually work our way to the outdoor seats at the front and stay on for as long as possible. This is definitely a cheaper way to tour the Grand Canal than a water taxi and, after passing under a variety of famous bridges, we motor right on out across the lagoon and back around to the Piazza San Marco. Photo opportunities abound and we take full advantage of the glorious day in the knowledge that the weather may change for the worse soon.

We visit the Gallery Ca' Pesaro, which is housed in a huge *palazzo*, and which has a fantastic exhibition of sculpture, painting and glass, including Klimt and Rodin, together with some Italian artists we have never heard of. It's well worth a visit - the gallery also has a groovy cafe that faces out through open arches onto the Grand Canal.

A longer waterbus trip takes us out across the lagoon to the island of Murano, famous for its manufacture of colourful glass. Murano has quiet canals and a very laid back and peaceful feel compared to the hustle and bustle of Venice. You can visit its glass museum, go to demonstrations of glass blowing and glass manufacture, and shop in endless glass-filled shops selling everything from the allegedly arty to bright tourist tat.

We do none of the above. To be honest, neither of us particularly likes any of the vast array of glass objects we see on our wander through the streets and canals of Murano.

It is such a joy to visit Venice with a bit more money than we had back in 1980 and to be able to stay in such a fantastic location as we are. We feel that this time we have really got around the city and sampled what it has to offer. In the evening, a five-minute stroll takes up from the quiet backstreet we inhabit to a busy thoroughfare with a few nice little *trattorias* to try - not surprisingly, the sea bream is particularly good.

We visit one such establishment two nights in a row and get chatting to the waiter. He appears to be comfortably multilingual and manages to strike up a three-way conversation which also includes a young Spanish couple at a nearby table. He laments the fact that the season has been a disappointing one, mainly due to the lack of visitors from the Far East. Apparently, visitors from Scotland are all very well, but they don't spend as much on alcohol as their Japanese equivalents. That's the first time I've heard that one.

During our meal, Fiona has been lamenting the fact that she has virtually lost her sense of taste. After dispensing a withering look in my direction, when I wittily respond that her dress isn't all that bad, the penny (which might also be likened to a large and unstable elephant in the room) begins to drop.

When we get back to our apartment, she fishes out our Covid

test kits, does the necessary, and I rapidly do likewise. Her test strip shows a reasonably faint positive red line. Mine comes up negative. Fiona follows suit with a negative test the next day.

I'm still not clear whether we have actually been in denial, or that we're just stupid. We have been convinced that we both have annoying head colds, neither of us having tested positive for Covid at any time previously during the pandemic. We have undoubtedly had the same bug, and Fiona looks to be just coming to the end of it, whilst I am a couple of days ahead of her.

There is a sinking feeling of guilt that we have been carrying on as normal, albeit wearing face masks on public transport, whilst almost certainly positive for the virus. We assuage this feeling a little by remembering how many passengers on the cruise ship were openly coughing and spluttering, and that we were amongst the few non-crew members who wore masks on board.

On the plus side, our own Covid experience has been manageable, though we have tired more quickly than usual, and there has been no trepidation as to how bad the illness will get. We are both on our way out of the woods by the time we realise we have entered them.

The dreaded event has finally happened, and we appear to have come through without suffering too bad an experience. Some classic symptoms persist for a few days afterwards, but these are an annoyance rather than a hindrance or a concern.

Getting around by the *vaporetti* is a great way to see Venice, but they can be very crowded and are a favoured haunt of pickpockets. On one journey, we are preparing to disembark to return to our apartment, when Fiona senses trouble. She reaches down to find a woman's hand has unzipped her shoulder pouch and her iPhone is halfway out. The hand withdraws and its owner melts into the crowd, but it is a salutary lesson on personal security for us.

I'm apparently beginning to get a bit of a reputation for being hare-brained. I can't think why. As we prepare to leave the Ca' dei Cuori apartment to catch the *vaporetto* to the railway station for our train to Verona, we have a last look around. Fiona spies something slim and red peeping out from the side of a cushion.

My passport is tucked away down an armchair, only just visible. I am favoured with yet another withering glare - leaving that behind would have complicated life somewhat!

Helpful Hints: Venice

Take the time to explore Venice properly - we would suggest a minimum of five days. Select your accommodation carefully, as surprising gems are available and early booking can secure them at a more reasonable price.

Buy vaporetto passes when you arrive the main ticket office is right in front of the railway station. Hopping on and off the water buses is a great way to get about once you've worked out the various routes!

Astute use of the vaporetti, especially on a beautiful day, can make for a much cheaper "tour" of Venice than the expensive water taxis.

Visit a couple of galleries/museums during your stay. The Gallery Ca' Pesaro is a hugely impressive building and exhibition space and houses fantastic exhibits. See details at:

capesaro.visitmuve.it/en/home/

Beware of pickpockets, especially on public transport. Vigilance is required in addition to sensible means of carrying your valuables.

CHAPTER 41: VERONA

Another comfortable train ride, complete with the most minute complimentary coffee each, takes us to Verona Puerto Nuova railway station, then a taxi drops us at our apartment.

Our room in the Lady Verona residence is like a large hotel room, with a communal kitchen outside, which no one else seems to use. We also have a small stone balcony which affords a great view of the river and of the Castelvecchio (Old Castle) especially when it's floodlit at night. The residence's advertised roof terrace requires mountaineering skills (ok - climbing a steep and narrow spiral staircase) so we only make the trip once, though admittedly the view is pretty good.

Verona's old town proves to be eminently walkable, and we take in some of the major sites in the glorious sunshine. The famous Roman amphitheatre - the Verona Arena - is at the end of its season, but we visit the interior anyway and watch preparations for the final event of 2022, which is some sort of musical.

The Arena is at one end of the massive Piazza Bra, the showpiece main square in Verona, which features lots of large cafes and an attractive small park in the middle. Apparently, the Piazza Pants is a bit further south, but we didn't make it that far down.

Everywhere we walk in the city seems to have beautiful, aged buildings and there is a genuine air of romanticism, entirely in keeping with Shakespeare's choice of the city as the setting for Romeo and Juliet. In the evening, every side street seems to offer a selection of appealing bars and restaurants. It's noticeable how frequently we see two women dining out together here - subjectively, it seems more common practice than it is back home.

Mention of Romeo and Juliet of course brings us to one of the city's premier tourist magnets - Giuletta's House, complete with the legendary balcony. Now Shakespeare's play was inspired by the Arthur Brooke poem, *The Tragicall Historye of Romeus and Juliet*, which was published in 1562. The poem was in turn inspired by older works by Italian writers, which told the story of Romeo and Giuletta, and the deadly feud between the families Montecchi and Capelletti.

The house was once inhabited by the Cappello family - a name similar to the Italian version's Capelletti - and dates back to the 13th century. However, the famous balcony wasn't added until the 20th century. At the top of the courtyard stands a statue of Giuletta. For some reason it is thought to be good luck to rub Giuletta's right breast, to ensure the rubber's good fortune in love.

When we make a (brief) visit, a queue snakes back from the rugby scrum of the courtyard outside the house, and below the legendary balcony, back into the street beside the Piazza delle Erbe, as people patiently wait in line (so they can't be Italian) to fondle the unfortunate statue's breasts. The visitors don't seem to really discriminate between right and left, as long as the essential photo is snapped. The poor girl must have the most rubbed knockers in Italy.

It is a little bewildering to see large numbers of people who are desperate to fondle the boobs of a statue of a woman who didn't exist, outside a house she didn't live in (because she didn't exist), under a balcony she didn't appear on (because she didn't .... you get the picture), in order to gain some luck in love.

Bear in mind that the fictional Juliet fakes her own death, Romeo believes her to be dead and so he takes his own life in Juliet's tomb, then she wakes to find Romeo's corpse beside her and kills herself. Lucky white heather.

Nevertheless, thousands of people apparently write to Juliet every year seeking advice on matters of the heart. A team of volunteers ensures that every letter is responded to. Proof, if it were needed, that romantics really can be incurable. As Tina Turner once melodically observed: "What's Love Got To Do With It?"

At one end of the Piazza delle Erbe is the incredible Palazzo Maffei, which now houses a private collection of every type of art, ancient and modern, assembled at an eye-watering cost, and open to the general public. It is one of the most amazing gallery/museum spaces either of us has ever experienced. Even the rooftop sports an impressive array of statuary, as well as a vertigo-inducing view of the Piazza below.

Although you can walk to most places of interest in the old town, we decide to also take the city bus tour, which shows us places we might not otherwise have reached. The tour is unusually excellent, and it confirms the view that Verona is probably the most attractive of the Italian cities we've visited (leaving aside Venice, which is entirely unique). It seems like the ideal destination for a weekend break, particularly at this time of year when tourist numbers have scaled down a little, though the place is still busy and buzzing.

We also hop off the bus to visit the beautiful and quite large 16th Century Giusti Palace and Gardens. We spend our time there in the gardens which are regarded as one of the finest examples of an Italian Renaissance garden. The Giusti family has owned the gardens since they were planted in 1580 and indeed were authorised to augment their family name to "Giusti del Giardino" due to the gardens' importance.

As I pay the entry fees at the small kiosk near the entrance, I'm glad that one of the features of my Starling debit card is that it instantaneously flashes up the details of a transaction on my phone screen. This prevents me from erroneously paying Euros 75 for entry, as opposed to the correct sum of Euros 20, for the two of us - you have to keep your wits about you with these Italian aristocrats!

The gardens are lovely to wander through in the late afternoon sun, on paths winding upwards past the fountain and the maze to the upper sections, which have been hewn from the overhanging rock. The small classical folly/pavilion makes a great spot for a photo, with the backdrop of the beautiful city of Verona.

Verona also seems like it would be a great place to go to university. Between studies, you can even take yourself along to the Marcantonio Bentegodi Stadium to watch former Hibs player Josh Doig playing for Hellas Verona - a club founded in 1903 by college students together with their Greek professor. A Hibs player moving to Italy's Serie A. Now that's a romance made in heaven!

Helpful Hints: Verona

A short train journey from Venice, Verona is equally well worth a 3 to 4-day visit.

Whilst walking gets you to most of the well-known sights, the city bus tour is one of the best we have taken.

At the risk of being branded a romance-free soul, all the Romeo and Juliet stuff is a transparent tourist trap built on, well, nothing really. Expect to make short and crowded visits - it has to be done!

Go up the funicular railway at Castell San Pietro. The views of the city from the top are stunning. See:

https://verona.com/en/verona/castel-san-pietro/

Verona really does have a romantic atmosphere and going out to the old town's bars and restaurants in the evening is a real pleasure.

CHAPTER42: PALAU

After a short flight from Verona to Olbia in Sardinia, we are picked up by a driver who takes us up the long and winding road from Olbia airport to Palau, on Sardinia's famed Costa Smeralda. This area on the north coast of the island is famous for its sparkling turquoise waters and fine sandy beaches.

Our first impressions are very positive - contrary to the weather forecast it's a beautiful day. Sardinia welcomes us with a wide, expansive vista of green hills, small bare mountains, sea, and islands, and the odd intriguing fortification visible on hilltops from the road.

Our driver hurtles along, at all times around three feet behind the car in front, even when it is the only vehicle in sight on our side of the road. There is no possibility of overtaking due to the oncoming traffic on the endless tight bends. I nod off intermittently, which is probably a stress-mitigating reaction to our hairy journey. The experience serves to confirm that our decision not to hire a car for our time in Sardinia is the right one.

We are finally safely deposited at our apartment - the Charme House - which is situated even further up the steep hill rising from Palau's port than we had anticipated. As the friendly Gabriella shows us round the small but very attractive living space, I immediately drift over to what attracted me to this place initially, the fabulous view from the large balcony down to the port and across the sea to a number of large islands - it is idyllic.

Ferries ply their way to and fro across the stretch of water between Palau and the island of La Maddalena. Small craft endlessly sail busily around, and the view of Palau's marina and port changes subtly with the light as the day progresses.

Once we have organised ourselves a bit, we walk down the steep winding road from the apartment, past the Grand Hotel and on towards the port, to explore. On the way down, it becomes apparent that a lot of concrete has been used in the building of Palau. The terracotta-coloured buildings, which appear quite attractive from a distance, are fashioned from concrete. Close up, they are painted rather drab shades of brown, orange and ochre.

We take a walk along the town beach which is OK, but unspectacular. It definitely doesn't fit the descriptions of the Costa Smeralda beaches we have read about in the guide books.

When we reach the waterfront, we sit on a rather jaunty blue concrete bench and take in the scene. The main feature of the port is a large, pale yellow painted concrete Italian police station, which looks to be of 1960s vintage. On the short trip down to the marina, Edinburgh residents might think of a cross between 1980s Wester Hailes and 1960s Portobello. Neither is a compliment.

There are none of the restaurants or bars we expect of a Mediterranean marina, just bare dockside and a couple of small, nondescript offices. One of these buildings houses the Centre for Psychology. Three or four sad looking restaurants huddle together a couple of hundred metres away, behind a large car park and a children's playground. None of them look worth a visit.

After a bit of a silence, the conversation goes something like this.

Fiona: "Palau is a bit of a hole, isn't it?" Me: "Yes, it is."

Bear in mind we have had to dodge the extravagantly dog poo smeared pavements beside the rubbish strewn scrub areas on the way to the attractively spray-painted waterfront. As we sit on our blue concrete bench a number of glum looking, mostly German (from overheard snatches of their conversation), couples and families trudge past us along the dockside.

We can only presume these poor souls are in transit between

their places of holiday residence and the Centre for Psychology, where they have arranged counselling appointments, during which the conversation might begin something like:

Tourists: "Why, oh why have we decided to come to this dump for our holidays?"

Therapist: "Why do *you* think you've decided to come to this dump for your holidays?"

Normally, in the course of one of our longer trips, we arrive at a destination which proves to be a little ill-judged. This is generally at my instigation and against Fiona's better judgement. Palau is no exception, and in fact it could be said to take the biscuit in this regard. Must listen to Fiona in future.

After doing a very large shopping at a SPAR on the outskirts of town, we persuade the shop manager to arrange for a car to take us home, at the rate for a normal taxi. We spend a couple of days without crossing the threshold of our apartment. The first is a day of torrential rain, the second starts badly weather-wise but brightens up in the late morning. We book a trip around the islands of the Maddalena Archipelago online and turn up sharp to join an already busy boat.

Bad weather threatens again but moves on, and we have a lovely day trip around the islands of La Maddalena, Spargi, Santa Maria and Budelli. This finally lets us see why the Costa Smeralda is so named and has the reputation it has. Spargi, in particular, has idyllic beaches with white sand, blue-green crystal-clear water, and unusual rock formations. It rivals any of the beaches we've been to anywhere in the world for natural beauty.

Spargi lies in the Strait of Bonifacio between Sardinia and Corsica. It is uninhabited, though legend has it that Natale Berretta, an infamous alleged bandit in the 19th Century, successfully hid out in Spargi's almost impenetrable interior. He eluded searchers until his name was apparently cleared, and he was able to return to Sardinia with his family.

It's a bit windy, but some brave souls take the opportunity to swim in the sea at each stop the boat makes. We settle for admiring the scenery and taking lots of photos. The well organised trip includes the option to buy lunch - surprisingly good seafood pasta brought to our seat. We begin to appreciate Sardinia a little more.

Next morning, we are picked up outside the Charme House twenty minutes late for a transfer by car, which had obviously forgotten us, to take us to the ferry terminal at Santa Theresa.

At the terminal we board the slightly aged-looking ferry for the fifty-minute trip to Corsica, finally leaving Italy behind for country number six: Vive la France!

Helpful Hints: Palau

I hesitate to say of anywhere just don't go there, but the town of Palau itself has little to offer, in our view.

It does, however, provide a jumping-off point for some nice boat trips to the nearby islands of La Maddalena.

The Charme House and its view were everything we'd envisaged. However, staying up the steep hill from the port means a long winding climb (there is no direct way up and down) to your accommodation, unless you get a Euros 10 taxi that is!

CHAPTER 43: BONIFACIO

We've wanted to visit the island of Corsica ever since Fiona's sister Pauline showed us photos and a video from their holiday there, somewhere in the region of thirty years ago. A trip to the Mediterranean's fourth largest island (after Cyprus, Sardinia and Sicily) has been on our travel destination wish list for all that time.

As we traverse the Strait of Bonifacio between Sardinia and Corsica, on the somewhat beat-up looking Moby ferry, Bonifacio makes its presence felt from some way out. First the chalky white limestone cliffs of the south coast of the island come into focus, then so do the huddle of buildings teetering improbably on those clifftops, all set against a dramatic mountain backdrop.

The closer the ferry approaches, the more stunning and impressive the city of Bonifacio becomes, until we are right under its old Citadel, peering out from the deck rail to try to see a break in the cliffs which will mark the entrance to the harbour.

The choice of our location on this large island has been heavily influenced by the fact that Fiona gave me a painting of Bonifacio by one of our favourite artists, Tom Watt, for our 40th Wedding Anniversary back on 1st May 2022. We then decided we'd like to see the place in the flesh, rather than head for the bigger cities like Ajaccio or Calvi.

We sail into the harbour past the huge mediaeval fortifications, past the rusted metal winches which were used to pull chains across the harbour mouth, to discourage enemy ships during

World War Two, and on into what must be one of the most attractive ports in the Mediterranean. Down in this part of the city, the sailing fraternity rules.

Fiona has come up trumps again as far as accommodation goes. We are in an hotel right at the far end of the port called the Roy d'Aragon, and she has secured a room which must have the biggest and best balcony space of any on the waterfront. It has a fabulous view of the port and the towering citadel, the latter eccentrically floodlit at night - garish mauve with an intermittent flashing red. The light show is complemented by the bright green pharmacy sign below the old walls, which is always showing the wrong time and temperature.

We decide to get some dinner quite close to our hotel in the port. We opt for a pizzeria by the waterside, but when we sit down it's apparent that the space is full of smokers and so cigarette smoke. We suggest to the owner that we could maybe move across the small street to the other section of the restaurant which is almost empty. "Is the same!" he shouts over his shoulder, which is as close to "Please bugger off!" as it needs to be, so we do.

A local man later informs us that smoking is so popular that Corsican restaurants get around the anti-smoking laws by pretending they are open air spaces then rolling down transparent plastic sides. All the smokers can then enjoy their fags fully and constantly throughout your meal.

Later in the evening we walk past the nearby Caravelle Restaurant, which looks to be extremely expensive. It also has a semi-outdoor bar and club area, where apparently older sailing gentlemen, weather beaten and slightly roguish looking, can fraternise with attractive younger women, whilst the beat goes on and the lasers pulse and play. We retire to bed.

In the morning, we meet the rudest person we have yet encountered in the course of our trip. She has the fairly simple job of selling the one price tickets for the little tourist train, which is the cheapest way to wind your way up the precipitous road to the Citadel and the old town, which loom over the entrance to the port. She manages to make this simple task difficult and unpleasant.

Perhaps she is fed up with the endless boat and bus loads of aged German tourists who appear at her kiosk window a number of times each day, looking to be whisked up to the Citadel in the miniature trains. In any event she might like to consider more sympathetic forms of employment, like Abattoir Attendant, or Edinburgh City Councillor.

Once we are up in the Citadel within the old city walls, it almost becomes like A Tale of Two Cities. Not quite London and Paris, but up the steep hill lie quaint mediaeval streets, nice bars and restaurants and apparently much more pleasant people. Oh, and absolutely breathtakingly spectacular views of the sheer limestone cliffs and the dazzling turquoise sea all the way over to Sardinia.

Sitting outside one tiny bar beside a church loggia we peruse the junk, sorry antique pieces, on show on the adjacent stalls. The bar owner sets these items out every day and runs these two sides of his business in parallel.

We ask for red wine. He has none. A French bar with no red wine. Beers? He hopes so and manages to tip the barrel far enough to get us two nice cold *Pietras*, Corsican beer which also comes, I later discover, in the form of an excellent amber brew with walnut.

The bar owner is gangly, eccentric, very friendly, and everything in sight is ancient, including the bar's tables, chairs, and lamps. When not serving customers, he flits about straightening up and adding to the objects which are for sale. He is immediately likeable and the ever-decreasing choice of drinks seems to do nothing to deter patrons as the place rapidly fills up.

Our experience is that French folk seem generally to be very friendly and convivial, and always engage in conversation when thrown together - our own deficiencies in the language department unfortunately block many of those possibilities.

We shop at a yet another SPAR down in the port, on our tour

of the SPARS of Europe. SPAR stores in Corsica and Venice really seem to be a bit of a cut above their equivalents back home, particularly in the quality of the produce which is on sale. Delicious plain and chocolate croissants baked and bought fresh every morning being a case in point in Bonifacio.

We go on two different boat trips whilst we are in Bonifacio. Conveniently, the excursions leave from the pier twenty metres from our hotel entrance. One trip goes along by the white cliffs to a couple of the Lavezzi islands, which have similar beautiful green-blue water to the Maddalena islands off Sardinia, and also feature their own intriguing rock formations, set against a glorious blue sky with fluffy white clouds.

The other route hugs the coast in the opposite direction, visiting a couple of large caves and some lovely small bays, one of which boasts a rock formation which is said to resemble Napoleon's helmet. Not tonight, Josephine....

There's nothing quite as relaxing as puttering along on the blue-green Mediterranean, with the sun's rays cascading down, as your little boat takes you from one beautiful and interesting vista to another. Portugal, Spain, Croatia, Italy, Greece, France - the sights may differ, but the feeling remains the same.

When we are not enjoying the sun and the breeze on the high seas or wandering about the confusing streets of the Citadel enjoying the fabulous views, we adjourn to our hotel balcony. From here we can survey the whole panorama of the marina and the Citadel at our leisure, and watch all the maritime comings and goings, with our refreshments of choice.

Some time is also spent out in the hot sunshine, trying to locate the exact spot on the waterfront at which Tom Watt must have set up his easel, when he executed his expert rendition of the view depicted in our painting. We conclude that some artistic licence has been employed, as Tom has made the scene look even more attractive than it is in real life. However, we finally settle on the nearest point possible and take a few photographs that are not too far away from an identical view.

Not a bad choice for our penultimate destination, and we are both very happy to have finally made it to Corsica, after years of talking about it!

Helpful Hints: Bonifacio

Bonifacio is easily reachable by ferry from Sardinia, and is a truly spectacular place. It's well worth considering as a destination, either as well as or instead of the more well know cities elsewhere on Corsica.

Staying down in the port area is fine, but the Citadel is lovely and offers much better bars and restaurants.

Bonifacio is also a great place from which to take tours along the southern coast of Corsica and out to the nearby islands.

The tourist train is an ideal, inexpensive way to shuttle between the port and the Citadel. It saves on taxi fares and on shoe leather!

The city provides a great taster for Corsica which encourages a further visit to explore more of this unique island.

CHAPTER 44: SOL DEL ESTE, MENORCA

It's a 5:00am start from Bonifacio, as we are picked up from our hotel by a driver to take us to the very basic airport at Figari. The driver covers the distance at breakneck speed, naturally, reassuringly indicating that there are few cars on the road at this hour. However, he mentions that the main problem is presented by encountering wild boar or wild cows wandering on the road in the dark. We spend the trip scanning the roadside for possible incursions by kamikaze beasts.

To call the airport at Figari basic is actually paying it a bit of a compliment. We finally twig that we have to walk back outside the terminal and re-enter the building at another door to reach our gate. An error is made at the security point, and a poor woman has to empty every item from her carry-on suitcase, in full view of the other passengers waiting in the cramped room. The security officials think they have spotted something suspicious in her luggage, but they don't seem to be sure whether it was in her case or in someone else's.

Our flight from Corsica lands in Bordeaux. An odd feature of Bordeaux airport is the plethora of signs threatening prosecution for assaults on airport personnel. Whether this is because such events are commonplace, or because a single event has taken place and this is the reaction of airport management, is open to conjecture.

We arrive in Mahón on time, clear Menorca airport quickly and pick up our hire car. We are staying for one night at the Barcelo

Hamilton hotel, which is just along the road from our apartment in La Gardenia, in Es Castell. We arrive just behind a large party of Spanish folk who are being greeted at Reception with glasses of cava and much welcoming chat. It takes us half an hour to get checked in.

We arrive around the corner in Calas Fonts for a lovely dinner in Sa Punta with Pauline (Fiona's sister), and her partner Paul, with seven minutes to spare. Not too bad, I suppose - it has taken us nearly six weeks to get here. Sa Punta is a new favourite, due to the good atmosphere, friendly staff, excellent food and wine, and the restaurant's great location at the entrance to Calas Fonts harbour.

The next day, we are fortunate enough to go on an unusual boat trip from Mahón harbour, on the Pascual Flores, an old salt boat launched in 1917, which was discovered mouldering in a port on the Welsh coast but has now been fully restored. The weather is glorious, and we spend three hours sailing out of Mahón harbour, pottering around on the high seas, then sailing back in.

The part of the trip outside the harbour is under sail only, which is fantastic. There is just enough wind to fill the sails, with not too much rocking and rolling. The crew members are mostly in their late teens with a couple of 20-somethings in charge. They work incredibly hard in small teams to perform the tough manual labour required to raise all the huge sails, which takes around thirty minutes in total. Then they have to take them down again as we come back into port!

Thanks to the very handy Marine Traffic app that Pauline has shown to Fiona, we know that just outside the harbour mouth lurks the cruise ship MSC Orchestra, at anchor off the La Mola headland, as it is presumably too large to come right into the cruise ship terminal. We sail by it as it ferries endless boatloads of people ashore in tenders so that they can visit Mahón.

Our own Mediterranean cruise earlier on this trip was on one of the Orchestra's sister ships the MSC Fantasia. There is a satisfying resonance for us from the presence of the Orchestra towards the end of our current trip. Back in 2020, it was the ship on which we had booked a cruise to South America, which fell victim to the pandemic. Five iterations of the cruise later, we accepted the Eastern Mediterranean cruise on the Fantasia, so there is a certain pleasing symmetry to events.

We also take a look around two very interesting replicas of Spanish galleons which are visiting Mahón. The original of one of these ships was the first to circumnavigate the globe. The day is very hot and humid and the temperature seems to rise by about 10 degrees with each deck we descend on these impressive ships, whose next port of call is Valencia.

It's Saturday evening, which we always try to spend in the buzzing city of Mahón, so we take the new lift up the cliffside from the port and start to climb the steep streets towards the cathedral. We are heading for a bar/restaurant we know quite well, and I can already taste the large gin and tonic, with copious ice, which awaits.

We turn the final corner to see to our dismay that La Bodega is closed and shuttered. There are no chairs and no tables in their normal places in the square in front of the cathedral. There is, however, a black and white cow in a small pen. And a police officer. Fiona catches up with me.

"Oh God, you were being serious. There actually is a cow," she observes. "and there's a policeman guarding it." There appears to have been some sort of agricultural show in the square, which is now winding down. No other livestock are in evidence.

An elderly lady strolls past pushing an alert-looking West Highland Terrier in a pink pram. We look around, wondering if we have stumbled into an episode of Doctor Who. Or perhaps Monty Python. Disoriented, we flop into chairs at the nearest bar, where we spend the rest of the evening eating surprisingly good traditional tapas and discovering a new, crisply sparkling cava.

The weather in Menorca is surprisingly hot and humid for mid-late October. We have been so fortunate on this trip, with only really two days of rain in nearly seven weeks. Even the locals here are commenting on the extended summer and the high temperatures. The heat and humidity are a bit sapping, so we get out on the water at every opportunity.

A trip across the harbour on the Yellow Catamaran takes us once again to Isla del Rey, with its restored military hospital, and the Hauser and Wirth Gallery, gardens, and sculpture trail. Although the beautiful gallery space is lovely and cool, we don't linger for too long, as the exhibition is a bit repetitive and, um, boring really. This gives us more time to sit outside the island's La Cantina restaurant, under the tree cover which gives us some shade, for a long and leisurely lunch in the balmy conditions.

As I've mentioned previously, despite the number of times we've been to the island, we always manage to do something new on each visit.

The *Cova de s'Aigua*, in the region of Ciutadella on the west side of the island, is a natural subterranean cave which occupies an area of around 2500m². It boasts a beautifully floodlit underground lake, which complements the weird and wonderful natural rock formations and the stalactites which hang overhead at various points in the easy-to-walk tour. The lake also features some strategically placed human bones which enhance the already excellent photo opportunities.

Our guide is a hugely knowledgeable about the geology and archaeology we are seeing, and he puts the information across in an engaging manner. We try to follow his Spanish flow, and he supplements this by explaining some of the highlights in English.

The Quarries of *S'Hostal* (better known as *Lithica*), also in the region of Ciutadella, are also well worth a visit. The *marés* stone of the quarry has provided the raw material for many structures in the west of Menorca.

Unlike most quarries, *Lithica* has not simply been left as an unsightly scar on the island's landscape, following stone production ceasing in 1994. The non-profit private foundation

Laetitia Sauleau Lara has intervened. An amazing maze has been built, a huge semi-abstract but recognisably human form towers over it, and large areas of the old quarry have been tastefully given over to the addition of a wide variety of plant life.

"A quarry reconceptualised as a type of unintentional architecture" is one description of *Lithica* which sticks in the mind as being particularly apposite. It's somewhere else we've been meaning to visit for some time, and we are very happy that we have now experienced this unique feature of the island.

We have two nice excursions to Es Castell and Es Grau for lunch with our old friend Jean, who now lives permanently in Cala'n Porter, about 30 minutes from Sol del Este. Jean was instrumental in us first visiting Menorca for a family holiday at Binixica way back in 1993, and in us learning of La Gardenia, where she also had an apartment for a number of years.

Our final evening here is traditionally spent up the road at Ignacio's - the Cafeteria Sol del Este. Unfortunately, he has closed early for the season. However, that gives us the opportunity to watch a basketball match at the Pavello de Menorca, for the first time since 2019!

Hestia Menorca has had a good start to the season in Spain's third division, the LEB Plata, and the team is going for its fifth win in a row. It is finally back in its home arena, after the roof had sprung a leak. Fiona has become a fan too, and we enjoy a comprehensive 80-47 home win over Brisasol CB Salou. Definitely a big improvement on watching Menorca's matches from afar, on YouTube and Canal+, over the past three years!

A friend on the island, who is also a basketball fan, said to me before the season started that he thought the new regime at the club was like a *chiringuito*, rather than a professional club. *Chiringuito* roughly translates as someone saying they own a restaurant when in reality they only have a rickety burger shack on the beach. Results so far tend to indicate that he may be wrong - let's hope that the club can get back to their previous loftier perch in Spain's top two divisions before long.

Our final evening makes for a pretty good send off for a fabulous trip all round. Home to Scotland tomorrow, to a huge temperature drop, no sunshine and the dark nights fair drawing in....

CHAPTER 45: BACK TO THE FUTURE

So, there we were, and here we are!

My decision to retire a couple of years before the standard age of 65 has allowed us, to some extent, to turn the clock back forty years. The nature of Fiona's online business has also helped hugely to accommodate this, as she continues to work successfully on trains, buses, and ships, as well as in cafés, holiday apartments and hotels, aided by some sterling help on hand back in Edinburgh.

All the travel experiences in between have served to educate us, and to equip us better to have the kinds of trip we want to have at the stage in our lives we are currently enjoying. We know the kind of experience we like, and we know how to go about achieving it.

We got the train journey through Portugal and Spain, and the trip in Sicily and the Western Mediterranean, in before the unimagined hiatus and challenges presented by the Covid-19 pandemic.

Everyone's lives, behaviours and to some extent attitudes have been affected by the conditions and restrictions the world has been experiencing since early 2020. At one point during the difficult years of 2020, and most of 2021, it was hard to imagine travelling abroad at all in the foreseeable future.

Although we selfishly felt unfortunate to catch Covid during the cruise segment of our latest trip, other people's lives have been much more profoundly affected by the pandemic, especially in the early months before the immense effort involved in worldwide vaccination programmes had the time to take effect.

We've caught up with friends, particularly in Menorca, whose lives were already quite isolated, and we've seen the mental and physical health effects that the extreme isolation engendered by the pandemic can produce.

We now feel almost back to normality personally, though the travel industry, particularly air travel, remains somewhat unstable and quite unpredictable. Our daughter Kathleen and her fiancée Lewis have just arranged their honeymoon to Aruba later in 2023 for the third time, due to issues with airlines and hotels.

We still view travel to more far-flung destinations, such as South America and Japan, with caution, and we've decided we shall probably wait until early 2024 before looking seriously at the possibilities in those directions once again.

However, just getting back in the saddle (metaphorically speaking again!) has had a hugely beneficial effect on us both. A cloud has lifted which had previously obscured new horizons and exciting possibilities.

On the negative side, we are older, we have more aches and pains, and probably more anxieties (well, I do). We tire a little more quickly, and so we try to plan itineraries that allow us the time to chill and relax fully, and that cut out some of the avoidable stresses that we can predict. Sometimes this involves the outlay of a little more money, but we feel it's worth the added expense to us.

A recurrent theme we meet on our travels is our own part in the linguistic backdrop to the destinations we have visited. The Scots, and probably the British as a whole, have a reputation for being poor at learning foreign languages, and that inevitably cuts us off from the possibilities of interesting conversations, as well as just understanding where we are going and what is going on.

We've spent some time trying to learn Spanish, through a mixture of classroom and online learning resources. We can now generally get by in Spain, or other Spanish-speaking areas, a bit more comfortably than we can pretty much anywhere else that English isn't widely spoken,

However, back to daily Duolingo is a New Year resolution for 2023!

Our thoughts are now turning towards planning our next trip. Maybe Spain and possibly Portugal once more, with different destinations along the way to last time. Maybe Greece and its islands. We shall see.

There's a huge world out there, and so many places we want to see and experience. Safe and happy travels wherever you go!

ACKNOWLEDGEMENT

Many thanks to Fiona and Kathleen Reid, and Jo Boyce, for proofreading and editorial input. And to Jo Torrance for constantly telling me to get on with it!